the new vision
for the new architecture
czechoslovakia 1918–1938

Scalo

the new vision

for the new architecture

czechoslovakia 1918–1938

jaroslav anděl

contents

preface

This book does not seek to survey the modern movement in architecture in interwar Czechoslovakia, although such a publication is long overdue. Instead it explores the role of photography in mediating a vision of modern architecture. We have become acquainted with most buildings through photographs disseminated by means of the printed page, postcards, exhibitions, and film, and this mediation has shaped not only our understanding of modern architecture but also played an instrumental role in articulating and communicating the idea of modern architecture and modernity itself.

Used in both general and empirical senses, the concept of vision is central to this subject. On one hand, it designated the notion of architecture as a powerful tool for building a new world, on the other it was associated with specific visual characteristics such as simple geometric forms, asymmetrical composition, or radiating white planes and volumes. For this reason, the book has been conceived primarily as a visual statement, with the text playing a supporting role. This presentation is typological rather than chronological: instead of an evolution of architectural forms and an overview of the most significant buildings and architects, the book highlights the significance of architectural images co-created by both architects and photographers, and associated with individual building types.

As a consequence, a discussion of the modern movement's development and its international relations is limited to only a few examples, primarily to the work of Le Corbusier, the Russian Constructivists and Bauhaus, in spite of the fact that Czech architects drew on a variety of other sources, including Dutch, American, and Scandinavian architecture. As the concept of *moderna* [modern style] coined by Otto Wagner's students such as Jan Kotěra at the beginning of the 20th century indicates, the work of domestic architects in the first two decades of the 20th century also paved the way for the rise of the modern movement in architecture after World War I in Czechoslovakia.

One must not forget that besides the international style associated with the concepts of purism and functionalism (as well as with the term 'new architecture' used in the 1920s and 1930s), there were other architectural movements and currents that made the architecture of the interwar period a complex and multifaceted phenomenon. Neoclassicism, for example, was a prominent force, and its impact can also be seen in the work of modern architects. Decorativism was another influential current that included international trends such as Art Deco as well as local varieties, an attempt to create a national style in architecture after World War I. Besides these movements, there were also individuals whose work cannot be easily classified (with Slovenian architect Josip Plečnik as a prime example) and who also left their mark by contributing to the richness of the period's architecture.

However, this pluralism did not last: it was the vision of modern architecture articulated by the international style that became a platform for further developments in the second half of the 20th century. This vision is now a component of modern heritage even if some of its concepts and principles have been redefined or refuted. It continues to shape our understanding of architecture and its role in the present world as contemporary architects face serious challenges and grope for a coherent vision.

The idea of this project occurred to me in the late 1980s, resulting in a paper given at the International Congress of Art History in Berlin in 1992. It also led to the project of an exhibition developed for the Fragner Gallery of Architecture in Prague and the Museum of Architecture in Frankfurt in 1991 (which did not materialize due to administrative changes in Prague). More recently, the subject of architectural photography and its impact on modern imagination has attracted the attention of contemporary artists and critics as a number of exhibitions, publications, and conferences testify. This growing interest also resulted in the present book (first published by Slovart in Prague in 2005) and the eponymous exhibition in London co-organized by the Royal Institute of British Architects and the Czech Centre in London, with the support of DOX, Centre for Contemporary Art in Prague.

In research and development of the publication, I was assisted by numerous individuals and institutions. I am indebted to Zdeněk Lukeš and Jana Tichá for reviewing my text and for a number of valuable suggestions and insights. I would also like to thank Claire Zimmerman, Miloslava Rupešová, Benjamin Frágner, Sylva Vítová, Josef Voříšek, Anna Fárová, Sylva Šantavá, Vladimír Šlapeta, Marie Benešová, Karel Kerlický and Jaroslav Kořán. I would like to acknowledge the assistance of several institutions and their professionals, including Jindřich Chatrný and Lenka Kudělková (Muzeum města Brna / Brno City Museum), Jan Hozák, Jiří Kröhn and Petr Krajčí (Národní technické muzeum v Praze / National Technical Museum, Prague), Antonín Dufek, Jiří Pátek, and Pavlína Vogelová (Moravská galerie v Brně / Moravian Gallery, Brno), Jan Mlčoch, Alena Zapletalová and Jarmila Okrouhlíková (Uměleckoprůmyslové muzeum v Praze / Museum of Decorative Arts, Prague), Viola Škabradová (Štencův archiv v Praze / Štenc Archive, Prague), Radomíra Sedláková (Národní galerie v Praze / National Gallery in Prague), and Anne W. Tucker and Marty Stein (The Museum of Fine Arts, Houston).

I would also like to extend my gratitude to Ladislav Pflimpfl (Czech Centre in London), Irena Murray and Rob Wilson (Royal Institute of British Architects), and Leoš Válka and Luca Ackerman (DOX, Centre for Contemporary Art) for supporting the eponymous exhibition project. I am very grateful for the contributions and important assistance of Juraj Heger, publisher, Richard Drury and Jana Steinerová, editors, in materializing the Slovart edition, as well as the expertise and assistance of the Grafický atelier Černý and Trico printers in Prague in improving the quality of printing in the Scalo edition. Last but not least, I am grateful to Walter Keller, publisher, and Teresa Go, editor, for their support and contributions to the realization of the Scalo edition.

Jaroslav Anděl

introduction

One of the most succinct definitions of architecture was given by Le Corbusier who described it as "the masterly, correct and magnificent play of masses brought together in light."[1] This passage first appeared in the series of Le Corbusier's articles on architecture in *L'Esprit nouveau* in October 1920, which were reprinted in Le Corbusier's book *Vers une architecture* (Paris: Crès, 1923). By foregrounding light and vision, the phrase contains a reference to neo-platonism, one of the most prominent philosophical traditions in the West. The neoplatonic import in Le Corbusier's writings is even more explicit in the following passage from the same paragraph: "[...] cubes, cones, spheres, cylinders or pyramids are the great primary forms [...] the most beautiful forms." According to Paul Turner, Le Corbusier owned a copy of Henri Provensal's book *L'Art de demain* (1904) which informed the architect's neoplatonic thoughts.[2] The quoted definition of architecture also highlights the role of perception and representation of architecture in architectural practice. These two closely interconnected issues imply the question "How is architecture mediated?" which is increasingly important, if not central, in the present age of new media and information revolution. In a broader historical context, it was the use of photography and photomechanical reproduction which paved the way to the current omnipresence of media and their role in both the reception and production of architecture. The great attention Le Corbusier paid to the photographic depiction of architecture in his publications, which is manifested in his use of such devices as cropping, retouching, scaling, and sequencing individual images confirms that the use of photography represents an important subject in the history of modern architecture that deserves much more study than it has received.[3]

This lack of attention does not mean, however, that proponents of the modern movement in architecture and photography did not reflect on the subject. In his article titled "The Largest Exhibition of Photographic Enlargements [Největší výstava fotografických zvětšenin]" (1940), the Czech avant-garde photographer František Čermák reviewed the exhibition *In Praise of the New Architecture* [Za novou architekturu], a survey of the most important works of modern architecture in Czechoslovakia, and highlighted the fact that these works were represented by photographic enlargements. The exhibition was unprecedented not only in its magnitude as it contained over one thousand works, but also in its timing. Originally planned by the Architects' Club for 1938, its realization was prevented by the conflict with Germany and the consequent dissolution of Czechoslovakia in 1939. Surprisingly, the exhibition took place in Prague during the German occupation in 1940, which, because of the Nazi regime's negative view of modern art, must be seen as an unprecedented event in the history of modern architecture in Central Europe. Since the exhibition consisted primarily of photographs, the exhibition also documented the collaborations between architects and photographers. Contemplating the implications of this fact, Čermák argued that the exhibition's title should have been *Photography In Praise of the New Architecture*.[4]

However, the point Čermák made more than sixty years ago was not taken seriously by architectural historians and critics or by historians of photography for decades. Architectural photographs, including the crucial period of the 1920s and 1930s, have been more or less overlooked as a subject of study by historians of both architecture and photography. For instance, scholars have written very little about an important body of work represented by Josef Sudek's pictures of modern architecture although they belong to the best examples of its genre. Sudek himself selected two architectural photographs for his monograph in 1956, *Stairs* (1928), a picture of the spiral stairs of the Brno Pavilion by Bohuslav Fuchs at the *Exhibition of Contemporary Culture in Czechoslovakia* in Brno in 1928, and *Gasworks* (1930), a picture of a gasometer of the Prague Gasworks.[5] Architectural photographs have been used most frequently as reproductions of architectural works and, in a few cases, as examples of one of many subject-matters in the history of photography. The significance of the exchange between the two media has been acknowledged only recently and there is still no monograph on the subject of photography and modern architecture available.[6]

By its very definition, architectural photography is an example of a symbiotic relationship of two different media, and thus represents an interesting case of media exchanges. The unfolding information revolution has fostered an interest in the interplay between various media and in the changes they carried into effect in the ways we produce, distribute and receive information. Consequently, new concepts and disciplines such as visual and media studies have emerged, transgressing traditional boundaries and divisions between various fields. While art historians have often specialized in one art form or medium, proponents of visual and media studies bring attention to complex relationships among various media and thus contribute to their better understanding. Here the concept of intermediality has become central to one of the fastest growing fields of social sciences.[7]

This book explores the significant body of architectural photography produced in Czechoslovakia in the 1920s and 1930s. In these important years, both architects and photographers saw themselves as participants in the creation of a new world, pursuing beliefs in social and technological utopias. Practitioners in the two fields shared and stimulated each other's vision, fostering interplay that consisted of mutual influences, parallels, and affinities.

This relationship was highly developed in Czechoslovakia where special conditions existed for the reception of the modern movement in both architecture and photography. The process of modernization as well as the creation of nation states and the rise of the middle class started later in Central Europe than in Western Europe. With its young middle class, the new Czechoslovak state eagerly embraced modern ideas and recognized in architecture a powerful tool for expressing its goals and ideals. For this reason, Czechoslovakia became one of the centers of the modern movement in architecture in the 1920s and 1930s as the quoted exhibition *In Praise of the New Architecture* testified. Its catalogue contained 1,206 examples of modern architecture that covered various trends and building types. These buildings represent a significant body of work that surpasses in its number and variety of building types architectural realizations in many other European countries.[8]

The medium of photography was also popular among Czech artists from the early 1900s, including leading painters and printmakers such as Alphonse Mucha, Vojtěch Preissig, and Josef Váchal. In the early 1920s, the new generation of artists associated with the avant-garde group Devětsil embraced photography and cinema as contemporary media that embodied the spirit of modernity, encouraging their use by artists and architects.[9]

While this confluence of architecture and photography in Czechoslovakia was fostered by specific regional circumstances, there were also broader historical processes of modernization that paved the way for the symbiosis of architecture and photography. Walter Benjamin noticed that the development of the technical forces of production in the 19th century "emancipated the constructive forms [Gestaltungsformen] from art, as the sciences freed themselves from philosophy in the 16th century." Benjamin concluded: "Architecture makes a start as constructional engineering. The reproduction of nature in photography follows."[10]

Although this observation comes from "Paris, Capital of the Nineteenth Century," a précis of Benjamin's unfinished *Arcades* project, one can hardly find a better introduction to a discussion of the relationship between architecture and photography in the modern movement. Two assumptions can be inferred from his remarks that will serve as the point of departure for our exploration of the subject. The first is that the modern movement embraced and celebrated 19th-century industrialization by developing its ideas and themes, the second, that this preoccupation foregrounded the media based on modern technology, fostering their cross-fertilization and development.

Constructivism, the avant-garde movement which originated in Soviet Russia and soon spread throughout Europe, played the central role in these developments. Obsessed with the machine, constructivism was bound to identify photography, film, and construction engineering with modern technology and progress. Constructivist artists and critics believed that new media and technologies would displace not only traditional art practices but art itself, which they wanted to replace with the more utilitarian function of design. While the constructivist doctrine was the kiss of death for painting, it inspired the boom of technologies associated with 19th-century modernization such as industrial architecture, photography and other communication technologies while informing the confluence of new media.[11]

The Czech avant-garde group Devětsil, which adopted the constructivist platform in 1922, celebrated photography and film in their exhibitions and publications. Founded in 1920, this association of avant-garde artists and architects also had a decisive impact on the two pioneers of modernist photography in Czechoslovakia: Jaroslav Rössler and Jaromír Funke. Significantly, one of the first discussions about the relationship between photography and architecture appeared in Devětsil's collection *Život; Sborník nové krásy* [Life; Anthology of the New Beauty], published in 1922. This important publication featured essays and photographs celebrating modern life and the achievements of modern technology; at the same time, it was introducing its readers to the international avant-garde. A number of its contributors, including Le Corbusier and Ozenfant, praised photography and film as potent agents of modern technology that promised to transform art.[12]

The essay "Photo Cinema Film [Foto kino film]" by Karel Teige elaborated this argument most forcefully, prefiguring later manifestos such as *Malerei Fotografie Film* (1925) by Moholy-Nagy and similar pronouncements by the Russian constructivists. Teige argued that the beauty of photography is identical with the "beauty of an airplane, ocean liner, and electric bulb."[13] In the same vein, the editor of *Život* and a leading architect of Devětsil, Jaromír Krejcar, criticized art for being "isolated from life and its rhythms" and hailed photography as "the only interpreter of the new beauty."[14] Krejcar's and Teige's view is reflected in the prominence given to photographs in *Život*, with the result that reproductions of paintings and sculptures alternated with enthusiastically displayed subject photographs of cars and ocean liners. Significantly, a photomontage by Teige, Krejcar, the architect Bedřich Feuerstein, and the painter Josef Šíma that highlights a car wheel and code words such as "life" and "new beauty" against a background of classical architecture, was used as the publication's cover.

Design for a Department Store in Prague (1922) by Jaromír Krejcar, which was reproduced in *Život*, also highlighted the theme of the automobile (as well as that of the skyscraper) and deployed elements of collage and photomontage in the tire advertisements and other signs and photographs of cars that were incorporated in and dominated the design. The *Život* cover and Krejcar's *Design for a Department Store in Prague* are some of the first instances of what would become the most popular iconographical motif in architectural drawings and photographs of the 1920s and 1930s: the car as an attribute and analogue of architecture.

The source of this conflation of architecture and the automobile can be found in the writings of Le Corbusier which appeared in the influential magazine *L'Esprit nouveau* published in Paris between 1920 and 1925. He argued that perfection resulted from the definition of standards and the consequent competition and selection of forms that was manifested by such different creations as the Greek temple or the automobile; he illustrated this point with photographs, for instance, with a picture of the Greek Temple in Paestum and a picture of a car. These two pictures, which appeared on the same page in the 10th issue of *L'Esprit nouveau* in 1921, invite comparison with the *Život* cover and suggest that the Czech artists drew on this juxtaposition.[15] But they collapsed the two subjects, the car and the Greek temple, into one picture by using their details and putting them together on a different background. Thus the result can be seen not only as a variation on the point made by Le Corbusier but also as a redefinition of the Swiss architect's concepts.[16]

This redefinition was achieved by identifying terms such as the new beauty, function, and poetry with modern media (photography and cinema) and by employing their devices (close-up and montage) or by directly adopting photography and cinema. Thus the point made by Le Corbusier was not only reinforced by the Czech artists but also changed: the message was transformed by using a new medium and by using it as the message. In the *Život* anthology, photography and cinema were celebrated as modern media not only through a number of essays but also directly by harnessing their devices in the anthology's layout and cover.

A similar shift can be seen in the reception and interpretation of concepts advanced by the international avant-garde—standardization, poetry, function, and construction—in the writings of the Devětsil artists. While according to Le Corbusier poetry resulted from standardization and purpose, the Czech artists saw poetry and construction as complementary and often as polar principles. In the manifesto "Our Base and Our Path: Constructivism and Poetism [Naše základna a naše cesta: Konstruktivismus a poetismus]," Karel Teige, a leading Devětsil theoretician, argued that "the psychological ability to experience special contrasts, which are almost paradoxically sharpened, is indispensable for man in the epoch whose heart seethes with contradictions" and that "life needs as much reason as poetry." Hence Teige claimed that the contrasts such as "nature-civilization, sentiment-intellect, imagination-rationality, freedom-discipline, construction-poetry, the public-private [...] do not destroy the value of individual elements but multiply it."[17]

The formative phase of the Devětsil program is evident in Teige's essay "Photo Cinema Film" which, in the period between the two wars, appears to be the first avant-garde manifesto that celebrated photography and cinema as the most contemporary art forms, predating similar statements by László Moholy-Nagy and the Russian constructivists. In this piece, the polarity of construction and poetry emerged in the use of such concepts as standards and purposefulness on one hand, and poetry (which was associated with Man Ray's rayograms) on the other. This suggests that it was the conceptual polarity of construction and poetry that enabled the Devětsil artists to synthesize various and often contradictory themes and ideas into a new aesthetic that characterized the Devětsil program.

This polarity of construction and poetry also informed the creation of a new art form or genre celebrating modern life that emerged in Prague in 1923. Inspired by pictorial weeklies, film, advertising, as well as by Dada and constructivist collages and photomontages, the picture poem, as the new form was called, combined collage, photomontage, and typographical design by juxtaposing fragments of words, photographs, maps, and other found material. If the concept of construction can be seen present in the geometric grid of picture poems, then poetry was associated with fragments of modern life, including planes, cars, ocean liners, skyscrapers, and popular art forms such as cinema and postcards.[18]

Between 1923 and 1927, picture poems were the favored medium among Devĕtsil members, who saw in them the very expression of the group's aesthetic. Although short-lived, the genre had a great impact on a number of art forms, including architecture and photography. For instance, Krejcar's influential *Design for the Olympic building* (1925–26), which became a prototype for residential and office buildings in Prague, can be seen as a picture poem in that it prominently displays words copied from vernacular architecture and juxtaposes them with other motifs common to the genre, such as cars, awnings, and radio antennae. In fact the contribution of the Devĕtsil architects can be characterized as an interpretation of Le Corbusier's Purism through the prism of their celebration of popular culture.[19]

One of the authors of picture poems was Jaroslav Rössler, the only photographer in the Devĕtsil group. His collages emphasized geometric elements and showed more affinity to the international constructivist movement than the work of other Devĕtsil artists. His picture poems reflected an interest in geometric abstraction that he also pursued in his photographs in the first half of the 1920s. While his first semi-abstract works such as *Opus I* (1919) were informed by cubism, several photographs from the early 1920s such as *Skylight* (1922–23) and the untitled photomontage of telephone wires from c. 1924 showed an affinity with the constructions by members of the Russian OBMOKhU (Society of Young Artists) group such as metal and wire structures.[20]

The early photographic work of Jaroslav Rössler includes other typical themes of constructivist architecture—radio and the tower structure. The artist had been an aficionado of technology in his teens; he built a radio receiver and made it the subject of numerous photographs. He also returned to the theme in several collages/picture poems. His photomontage entitled *Radio* (1923–24) intertwines images of a radio transmitter and a receiver, while the collage *Radio Marconi* (1926) integrates the image of a tower into a typographical design. Rössler's photographs of tower structures such as the Petřín Tower in Prague or the Eiffel Tower in Paris represent not only one of the earliest examples of constructivist photography but also indicate links between constructivist iconography and the 19th-century documentary photographs of engineering structures such bridges, towers, and exhibition halls. Rössler's picture representing a construction detail of the Petřín Tower in Prague (1923) appeared in *Stavba* in 1925 next to the article "The Beauty of Bridge Constructions [Krása mostních konstrukcí]" by Vilém Santholzer which praised the beauty of engineering structures.[21]

Rössler's work thus indicates how individual works are interconnected with contemporary discourse as well as with the tradition within its own medium, which was engaged in recording and publicizing the rise of new engineering structures and types. It also brings attention to the rise of new building types in the 19th century, a period in which urbanization and the growth of the middle and working class brought about new social, economic and cultural developments. And with these developments came new needs and demands which presented architects with unprecedented tasks and challenges. Over a relatively short period of time a number of new building types emerged which had not existed in previous centuries.

The American architect Henry van Brunt contemplated this subject in 1886: "The architect, in the course of his career, is called upon to erect buildings for every conceivable purpose, most of them adapted to requirements which have never before arisen in history. [...] Railway buildings of all sorts; churches with parlors, kitchens and society rooms; hotels on a scale never before dreamt of; public libraries the service of which fundamentally differed from any of its predecessors; office and mercantile structures, such as no existing conditions of professional and commercial life has ever required; school houses and college buildings, whose necessary equipment removes them far from venerable examples of Oxford and Cambridge; skating rinks, theaters, exhibition buildings of vast extent, casinos, jails, prisons, municipal buildings, music halls, apartment houses, and all other structures which must be accommodated for the complicated conditions of modern society. [...] Out of [...] the eminently practical considerations of planning must grow elevations, of which the essential character, if they are honestly composed, can have no precedent in architectural history."[22]

Each of the new building types played a specific role in the development of architecture and this role changed in time. Some building types were more important than others as they often not only followed particular functions and logistical requirements but also represented specific values and ideals. Enmeshed in larger social, economic and cultural environments, building types are emblematic of short- and long-term changes in modern society. For this reason, they enable us to examine the alliance between architecture and photography in a broader historical context, in particular with respect to the 19th century when the new medium of photography was widely used to document new construction projects. Thus the correspondence between the modern movement in architecture and 19th-century industrialization is revealed not only in the prominent role played by key building types but also in the process of the emancipation of new media and technologies described by Benjamin. The 1920s and 1930s accelerated both their emancipation and confluence, and brought them to a new level which is manifested in the large body of architectural photographs as well as in the use of cinema for representing architecture and the city. It is significant in this respect that the largest presentation of modern architectural photography of the period, the exhibition *In Praise of the New Architecture*, used the building type as its main organizing principle, starting with a survey of construction methods. Thematic organization based on building types had been common in architectural publications since the late 19th century, including architectural journals which often devoted single issues to specific building types. This publication follows a similar trajectory.

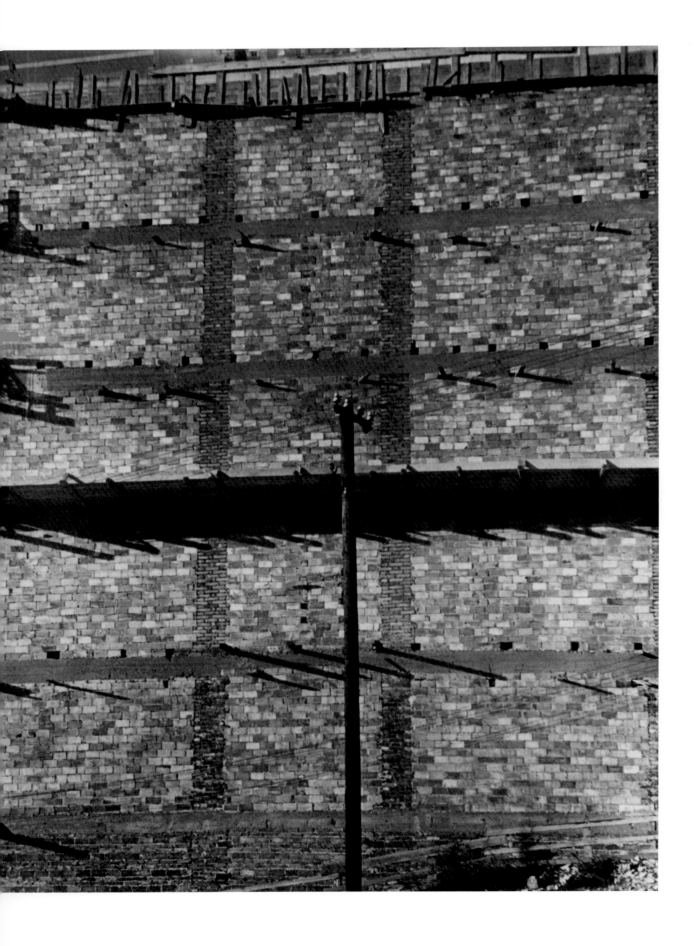

the poetry
of construction

The division of building into a skeleton and thin partitions that only insulate and divide, the negation of the structural walls results in a transformation of the appearance of structural character [...]

Karel Teige, "The Architecture of the Industrial Age [Architektura průmyslové doby]," 1925

the poetry
of construction

The binary concepts of construction and poetry—key words in the discourse of the Czech avant-garde movement associated with the group Devětsil—impacted the contributions of its members in different fields and informed the interplay between individual media in their work. The concept of construction referred to constructivism and evoked the movement's prominent source of inspiration: 19th-century engineering structures, such as the tower, which links the most symbolic example of engineering of that time, the Eiffel Tower, with the signature work of constructivism, Vladimir Tatlin's model for *The Monument to the Third International* (1920). *Život; Sborník nové krásy* made this connection explicitly by reproducing photographs of the two structures next to each other.[23] The motif of the tower structure was prominent in the work of Devětsil artists such as the architect Krejcar and the photographer Rössler, for example, in Rössler's *Untitled (Petřín Tower)*, c. 1923, and in Krejcar's design of the U.S.S.R. signpost at the Prague Sample Fairs (1928). However, each artist interpreted this constructivist emblem differently, which indicates that the concept of construction itself played a different role in the context of each artist's work. Rössler's photograph represents a construction detail which is conceived as an abstract composition of vertical and diagonal forms. The picture is closely related to the artist's series of abstract or semi-abstract compositions based on cardboard constructions from the same period. Unlike the Devětsil picture poems whose compositions combined the orthogonal grid of vertical and horizontal rectangular forms with representational elements, Rössler's photographic compositions were abstract and often included diagonal forms, a motif that became popular in the late 1920s.

While Rössler harnessed the motif of the tower structure to formal concerns such as abstraction, Krejcar referred explicitly to the romantic pathos of Russian constructivism and its political message manifested in agitprop. Krejcar's work also invokes the 19th-century pedigree of engineering structures more explicitly, although this lineage was not lost on Rössler as a number of his other photographs of tower structures, including the Eiffel Tower demonstrate.

Josef Hausenblas's photomontage *Untitled (Eiffel Tower)* (1928), which appeared in the 9th issue of *Review of Devětsil* in 1929, is another example connecting the central motif of constructivism to its 19th-century sources. Hausenblas's work was part of the Czech contribution to *Film und Foto* in Stuttgart in 1929, one of the most influential exhibitions of the interwar period. It seems to be both significant and ironic that in an exhibition that celebrated the power of the photographic and cinematic image, the Czech avant-garde was represented almost exclusively by architectural photomontages, not photographs, and that the work of pioneers of modern photography, Jaroslav Rössler and Jaromír Funke, was not included.[24]

The above comparison indicates that the relationship between construction and poetry and, consequently, the concept of construction itself, were interpreted differently by individual artists and had different implications in different media. There was an internal debate about this relationship within the Devětsil group, evolving from the initial enthusiasm about all forms of modernity to the gradual development and separation of individual concerns and the growing polarization of the two concepts. This increasing dichotomy emerged even in the group's architectural section, with architects such as Jaromír Krejcar, Evžen Linhart, Vít Obrtel, and

Jaroslav Rössler
Untitled (Petřín Tower, Construction Girder), 1923
Private collection

Jaroslav Rössler
Radio Marconi, 1926
Collage
Museum of Decorative Arts, Prague

Josef Hausenblas
Untitled (Eiffel Tower), 1928
Photocollage
In: *ReD* 2, no. 9, 1929, p. 292

Photographer unknown

Advertising Column for the U.S.S.R.
Pavilion, Prague-Holešovice, 1928
Architect Jaromír Krejcar, 1928
In: Karel Teige: *Práce Jaromíra Krejcara.*
Praha: Petr, 1933, p. 72

Jaromír Funke
Untitled (ESSO Power Plant, Kolín), c. 1930
Architect Jaroslav Fragner, 1929–32
Private collection

Jaromír Funke
From the series *New Architecture*
(ESSO Power Plant, Kolín), c. 1930
Architect Jaroslav Fragner, c. 1929–32
Private collection

Josef Havlíček who often incorporated into their work elements of vernacular architecture (including awnings, commercial lettering and signs, and neon advertisements) associated with the poetry of modern life on one hand, and architects and critics who emphasized the concepts of construction and function such as Teige and Jaroslav Fragner on the other. "Communication, organization, and hygiene in all floor plans; The economy of human work; Light and the lack of constraint; Treatment by sun and air; Glass, concrete, brick," demanded Fragner in his manifesto in 1925.[25]

Rationalist and functionalist views were also held by architects associated with the magazine *Stavba* [Construction], founded in 1922, such as Oldřich Tyl, and Oldřich Starý, and Ludvík Kysela who rejected the decorative architectural style popular in the late 1910s and early 1920s in favor of new architecture. The cover of the first *Stavba* issue is emblematic in this respect as it juxtaposed two stylized architectural motifs—a vertical construction void of any decoration with a façade decorated with a zigzag motif. In 1923 Teige joined the *Stavba* editorial board as its editor-in-chief and to a large extent became responsible for making it one of the leading organs of the new architecture in Europe.

The magazine followed a program which was outlined in the manifesto "Our View on Architecture [Náš názor na architekturu]," published as a conclusion to the report "Tenets of the New Architecture [Zásady nové architektury]" that summarized an international lecture series which took place in Prague and Brno in the late 1924 and early 1925 and in which leading figures of modern architecture (Adolf Loos, Le Corbusier, Walter Gropius, and Jacobus Johannes Pieter Oud) participated. The core statement of this manifesto saw parallels between "the process of creating new architecture" and "the production system of the modern machine" while recognizing in them "the same principles of rationalism, economy, and mathematical order."[26]

The mentioned works show that the depiction of construction evolved from abstract or semi-abstract compositions in Rössler's work and from the sociopolitical concerns in Krejcar's designs informed by Russian constructivism to more functional interpretations. Ten years after its first issue appeared, *Stavba* featured a photograph of a steel skeleton construction by Viktor Schück on its cover, demonstrating the lasting popularity of the construction theme. It is remarkably similar to a photograph of Jaromír Funke with an identical subject (steel structure) and composition (a diagonal view from below) from around 1930 and taken at the construction site of the ESSO Power Plant in Funke's native town of Kolín. Funke used the same composition in another picture of a construction taken at the same site which, instead of the steel skeleton, shows a structure of reinforced concrete and cinder blocks. The two pictures thus represents the two construction methods that have dominated modern architecture. In the late 1920s, the two construction methods, or more precisely, the industries which represented them, were competing with each other, as Karel Honzík described in the chapter with the telling title "The Invisible War [Neviditelná válka]" of his memoirs.[27]

The concept of construction implies the notion of process. This point was made by Jan Kučera in his film *Stavba* [Building] (1932–34) in which he sought to record the construction process of the first skyscraper in Prague, the General Pension Insurance Company Headquarters. (A similar film was also made on the construction of the Prague Electricity Board building). In collaboration with its architects Karel Honzík and Josef Havlíček, he also sought to communicate the principles of modern architecture by using specific cinematic devices and special effects, including time-lapse shots. Kučera's article "Cinema and Building [Film a stavba]," which appeared in the prestigious art magazine *Volné směry* [Free Directions], described his intention to explore the nature of construction as a process and its affinity with cinema: "This

Jaroslav Fragner
ESSO Power Plant in Construction, Kolín,
1930
Architect Jaroslav Fragner, 1929–32
Private collection

28. IX. 1930 ✕ 24

28. IX. 1930 ✕ 25

28. IX. 1930 ✕ 26

28. IX. 1930 ✕ 27

28. IX. 1930 ✕ 28

28. IX. 1930 ✕ 29

28. IX. 1930 ✕ 30

7

Photographer unknown

*Ceiling Slab Reinforcement, Prague Electricity
Board, Prague-Holešovice,* c. 1931
Architects Adolf Benš and Josef Kříž, 1927–35
Private collection

Jiří Lehovec
Vítkov Memorial in Construction,
Prague-Žižkov, 1929–30
Architect Jan Zázvorka, 1925–38
Private collection

counterpoint of the conception and the chaos which originates from materialization may give birth to a drama on the screen while a certain pathos is contained in individual images."[28] Unfortunately, the film was not finished and its footage was bought and used by Pierre Jeanneret (a cousin of Le Corbusier) and the Algiers Architects Association for the film *L'Architecture tchécoslovaque d'aujourd'hui* (1934).[29]

Specific interpretations of construction concepts characterized individual architectural schools and movements, including French purism, Dutch neoplasticism, Russian constructivism, and international functionalism, which impacted the centers of new architecture in Czechoslovakia: Prague, Brno, and Zlín. For instance, French purism received a great attention among the Devětsil artists in Prague, while the Dutch school influenced architects in Brno such as Bohuslav Fuchs and Jan Víšek, especially in the early and mid-1920s, and the Zlín architects were inspired by American industrial architecture.

For all its different readings and interpretations, a message of optimism transpires from photographs of construction and their various construction themes—a belief in progress, in building a better new world, to which both architects and photographers contribute with their work. The quoted exhibition *In Praise of the New Architecture* opened with the section titled "Construction Prerequisites and Possibilities of the New Architecture." The exhibition's organizers recognized "the rise and perfection of new construction systems and building materials as the main prerequisite of the new architecture"[30] and saw the need to develop a new field of construction research. Thus they found in new construction developments a link between the 19th century, new architecture and the architecture of the future: "Like in the last century, bold engineering constructions are harbingers of the future architecture today."[31]

Bohuslav Fuchs
Untitled, c. 1930
Brno City Museum, Architecture Collection

Bohuslav Fuchs
Untitled, c. 1930
Brno City Museum, Architecture Collection

Jan Kučera
Building, 1932–34
35 mm film frame enlargements
Private collection

e x h i b i t i o n s

What is exhibited here [...] are the means and results of science which are here to represent concepts of science and culture that are difficult to grasp and explicate.

Jiří Kroha, "How I Built the Exposition of Science [Jak jsem budoval expozici vědy]," 1928

In 1924 two important architectural competitions took place in Prague and Brno—the former was for the Prague Sample Fair Palace, the latter for the master plan of the regional fairgrounds in Brno. Both projects were completed with much publicity on the occasion of the 10th anniversary of the new state in 1928 and hailed as milestones in the history of modern architecture in Czechoslovakia, confirming the link between the new architecture and this building type rooted in the 19th century. This connection was especially evident in the case of the Prague Sample Fair Palace as it was located next to the older exhibition grounds created in 1891.

Designed by Oldřich Tyl and Josef Fuchs, the Prague Fair Palace was one of the largest structures of new architecture in Europe and had a great impact even on Le Corbusier. During his visit to Prague, the Swiss architect stated that "when I saw the fair building, I realized how I have to create large buildings, I, who have built so far only a few relatively small houses with a limited budget."[32] In his comments on the palace, Le Corbusier used such adjectives as "unique," "extraordinarily significant, ""impressive," "enormous," "grand"; but he also criticized it for consisting of "three or four buildings of different character which unsuccessfully intersect with each other." As a matter of fact, the structure represents a fusion of two related building types—the exhibition palace and the arcade.

One of the vintage photographs preserved of the Fair Sample Palace's interior was taken by Josef Sudek. It shows a staircase and an elevator shaft seen from a bird's-eye view. This approach, which was often associated with constructivism, is very different from the pictorialist and romantic style which characterized Sudek's work in the first half of the 1920s. However, the Fair Sample Palace lacked the revolutionary pathos of Russian constructivism which influenced some of the Devětsil architects such as Jaromír Krejcar. Other pictures of the palace's interior and exterior by an unknown photographer emphasize the grid of the building's structure and its huge scale. Their matter-of-factness corresponds with the functional and industrial nature of the building which represented a direction different from the lyrical style of the Devětsil architects and which made some critics link the building to the German movement of New Objectivity—*Neue Sachlichkeit*.[33]

In 1928 the regional fairgrounds in Brno opened with the *Exhibition of Contemporary Culture in Czechoslovakia*, the huge manifestation of a new national and cultural identity that celebrated the 10th anniversary of Czechoslovakia. It also symbolized the city's achievements in the field of new architecture, since the fairgrounds' master plan was authored by Brno architect Emil Králík, who also designed a cinema and café building at the fairgrounds. Among architects of individual pavilions were Josef Kalous and Jaroslav Valenta (Palace of Commerce and Industry), Bohuslav Fuchs (Brno Pavilion), Jiří Kroha (Mankind and Its Birth Pavilion), Bohumír František Antonín Čermák (Trade and Commerce Pavilion), and Vlastislav Chroust (Moravian Pavilion). Brno, a provincial city during the Austro-Hungarian Empire, became one of the centers of the new architecture in the period between the two wars.[34]

The exhibition examined the central position of science and education in modern society —a key feature whose significance has become ever more prominent—while highlighting the unique mission of architecture by making it the main medium of the exhibition's message and

Josef Sudek

Staircase in the Fair Sample Palace, Prague-Holešovice, 1932
Architects Oldřich Tyl and Josef Fuchs, 1924–28
National Gallery in Prague, Architecture Collection

Photographer unknown

Fair Sample Palace, Prague-Holešovice, 1928

Architects Oldřich Tyl and Josef Fuchs, 1924–28

National Gallery in Prague, Architecture

Collection

Photographer unknown
Fair Sample Palace, Prague-Holešovice, 1928
Architects Oldřich Tyl and Josef Fuchs, 1924–28
National Gallery in Prague, Architecture
Collection

ČLOVĚK A JEHO ROD

Photographer unknown
Regional Fairgrounds, Brno-Pisárky, c. 1928
Private collection

Photographer unknown
Palace of Commerce and Industry, Regional Fairgrounds, Brno-Pisárky, c. 1928
Architects Josef Kalous and Jaroslav Valenta, 1927–28
Private collection

Photographer unknown
Pavilion of Mankind and Its Birth, Regional Fairgrounds, Brno-Pisárky, 1928
Architect Jiří Kroha, 1927–28
Private collection

Hugo Táborský

Viewing Tower, Regional Fairgrounds,
Brno-Pisárky, c. 1930
Architect Bohumír F. A. Čermák, 1927–28
Private collection

Photographer unknown

Palace of Commerce and Industry, Regional
Fairgrounds, Brno-Pisárky, c. 1928
Architects Josef Kalous and Jaroslav
Valenta, 1927–28
Private collection

the message itself. The development of architecture and urbanism was presented by means of photographic enlargements and architectural drawings and models in the main pavilion, and was complemented by a separate pavilion called the New House (designed by Josef Havlíček) and the New House Colony, inspired by the Weissenhofsiedlung in Stuttgart which opened only a year earlier.[35]

The Exhibition of Contemporary Culture in Czechoslovakia and the new fairgrounds became a great success and the subject of numerous publications and photographs. Thousands of postcards depicting the fairgrounds from different angles replaced a traditional cityscape dominated by a Gothic cathedral with images of glass and reinforced concrete, creating a new symbol of the city, the new Brno.[36] The constructivist exhibition design authored by Jiří Kroha was an important component of the exhibition and contributed to its success. As photographs of the pavilions' interiors demonstrate, Kroha used the motifs of construction and the grid to organize interior space and emphasize the exhibition's highlights. He also employed this geometric vocabulary to create links between the fields of science, industry, art, and architecture.[37] In some cases, including the Pavilion of Mankind and Its Birth, Kroha's designs can be seen as monumental constructivist sculptures, symbolic statements in their own right whose optimistic message was communicated by their photographs. The exhibition organizers published a representative album of photographs *Výstava soudobé kultury v Československu,*

Hugo Táborský
Palace of Commerce and Industry, Regional Fairgrounds, Brno-Pisárky, c. 1930
Architects Josef Kalous and Jaroslav Valenta, 1927–28
Private collection

Photographer unknown
Exposition of Science, the Humanities and Technological Culture, and Higher Education; Exhibition of Contemporary Culture, Regional Fairgrounds, Brno, 1928
Architects Jiří Kroha (exhibition design), 1927-28; Josef Kalous and Jaroslav Valenta (pavilion), 1927-28

Photographer unknown

*Exposition of Science, the Humanities and
Technological Culture, and Higher Education;
Exhibition of Contemporary Culture in Czechoslovakia,
Regional Fairgrounds, Brno-Pisárky,* 1928
Architects Jiří Kroha (exhibition design), 1927–28;
Josef Kalous and Jaroslav Valenta (pavilion),
1927–28
Private collection

Photographer unknown ▷

*Exposition of Science, the Humanities and
Technological Culture, and Higher Education;
Exhibition of Contemporary Culture in Czechoslovakia,
Regional Fairgrounds, Brno-Pisárky,* 1928
Architects Jiří Kroha (exhibition design), 1927–28;
Josef Kalous and Jaroslav Valenta (pavilion),
1927–28
Private collection

Photographer unknown

Advertising Construction, Exhibition of
Northern Bohemia, Mladá Boleslav, 1927
Architect Jiří Kroha, 1927
Private collection

Photographer unknown

Dražice Cooperative Enterprises Pavilion,
Exhibition of Northern Bohemia in Mladá
Boleslav, 1927
Architect Jiří Kroha, 1926–27
Private collection

Photographer unknown

Mladá Boleslav Electricity Board Pavilion,
Exhibition of Northern Bohemia, Mladá
Boleslav, 1927
Architect Jiří Kroha, 1926–27
Private collection

Photographer unknown
*Mladá Boleslav Electricity Board Pavilion,
Exhibition of Northern Bohemia, Mladá
Boleslav,* 1927
Architect Jiří Kroha, 1926–27
Private collection

Photographer unknown

*Brewery A. S. Restaurant, Exhibition of
Physical Education and Sport in the
Czechoslovak Republic, Pardubice,* 1931
Architect Ferdinand Potůček, 1930–31
Private collection

Photographer unknown

*Stadium, Exhibition of Physical Education
and Sport in the Czechoslovak Republic,
Pardubice,* 1931
Architect Karel Řepa (with F. Potůček),
1930–31
Private collection

Photographer unknown ▷

*Automotive Pavilion, Exhibition of Physical
Education and Sport in the Czechoslovak
Republic, Pardubice,* 1931
Architect Karel Řepa, 1930–31
Private collection

Brno, květen–říjen 1928 [Exhibition of Contemporary Culture in Czechoslovakia, Brno, May-October, 1928] which documented Kroha's exhibition design in detail.[38]

Kroha employed constructivist devices such as the grid in his designs for the *Exhibition of Northern Bohemia* in Mladá Boleslav in 1927, which included the Main Pavilion, the Dražice Cooperative Enterprises Pavilion, the Mladá Boleslav Electricity Board Pavilion, and the Restaurant and Café Pavilions. The exhibition also included an exposition of modern architecture, while its pavilion design showed the distinct impact of Russian constructivism, providing an example of the confluence of exhibitions, constructivism and the development of the new architecture.

The Exhibition of Physical Education and Sport in the Czechoslovak Republic which opened in Pardubice in 1931 was another ambitious exhibition project that advanced the popularity of the new architecture. The author of its master plan was Karel Řepa, who also designed its pavilions, including the Pardubice Pavilion, the Automotive Pavilion and other industrial pavilions, as well as a racing stadium. Demolished after the exhibition in 1931, the pavilions are now preserved as photographs, including several pictures by Jaromír Funke and postcards which were widely distributed at the time.

Photographer unknown

Industrial Pavilion No. 11, Exhibition of Physical Education and Sport in the Czechoslovak Republic, Pardubice, 1931
Architect Karel Řepa, 1930–31
Private collection

Photographer unknown

Southern Bohemia Exhibition, Tábor, 1929
Architects Jan Chomutovský and Theodor Petřík, 1929
Private collection

Photographer unknown

Slovácko Region Exhibition, Uherské Hradiště, 1937
Architect Adolf Roštlapil, 1937
Private collection

Besides Prague, Brno, Pardubice, and Mladá Boleslav, there were a number of other regional exhibitions organized in the 1920s and 1930s. Almost every town with more than 20,000 inhabitants had its fairgrounds and exhibitions that often reflected its local traditions. For instance, the *Southern Bohemia Exhibition* in Tábor (1929) was complemented by an exposition of Czechoslovak military history, and the *Slovácko Region Exhibition* in Uherské Hradiště (1937) included ethnographic exhibits and agricultural products.[39] Widely publicized in their time, local fairs and exhibitions became memorable events in the development of both regional economy and culture while serving as a showcase for the new architecture. No other medium documented this union of exhibitions and new architecture better than the postcard. Produced in the thousands, the postcard advertised exhibitions as well as examples of the new architecture. Thanks to its popularity and mass distribution, this humble medium communicated the image of the new architecture to the general public and demonstrated the continuing alliance of architecture, photography, and industrial exhibitions.

Baťa
ZDRAVOTNÍ OBUV VYRÁBÍME VE 23 ŠÍŘKÁCH
DĚTSKÝ RÁJ A KRÁSNÉ STŘEVÍČKY PRO DĚTI
STŘEVÍČKY Z PRAVÉ JEŠTĚŘÍ A KROKODILÍ KŮŽE
Baťa
DŮM SLUŽBY

arcades and
department stores

Centropress

Baťa Department Store,
Prague-New Town, c. 1930
Baťa Construction Office (Jindřich Svoboda,
Consultant Ludvík Kysela), 1927–29
Private collection

Baťa [...] rightly recognized the significance of light and its impact as a means of advertising. The lower part of Wenceslas Square is illuminated by the intense light coming out of the new Baťa department store, and the brightly lit store windows attract the attention of passers-by with striking advertising.

Stavitel Editorial, "T. A. Baťa Co.'s Department Store in Prague; Illumination and Electric Fittings of Modern Buildings [Obchodní dům fy T. A. Baťa v Praze; Osvětlení a elektrická zařízení moderních budov]," 1930

arcades and
department stores

The arcade, a roofed store-lined street, originated in France and England during the first three decades of the 19th century. The fact that arcades flourished in Prague during the first decades of the 20th century and have continued to be popular to the present is testimony to the vitality of the building type. It also suggests its close connection to social and economic development, such as the market for luxury goods and the growing number of people who could afford them. Walter Benjamin, who chose the arcade as the subject of his monumental unfinished *Passagen-Werk,* explored arcades as a form emblematic of cultural, economic, and social change in European society driven by market forces.[40] He identified the railway constructions and the world exhibition halls as a technological harbinger of the arcades and underscored the significance of all these types for the advances of building in iron and glass—one of the sources of modern architecture. He also outlined various sociological and economic correspondences between photography and the railways, world exhibitions, and arcades grounded, primarily, in the expansion of the commodity trade and the harnessing of technology. He was among the first scholars to study how the arcade's dramatic architecture interpreted urban environment as a theater of consumption and how this creation of new forms of display and voyeurism introduced a new tradition of technological innovation.

In the 1920s and 1930s, this technological innovation continued in Prague's arcades such as the Alfa Passage (1928) designed by Ludvík Kysela, the Bondy Passage (1929–33) designed by Oldřich Tyl, and the Broadway Passage (1936–38) designed by Bohumír Kozák and Antonín Černý. They utilized new materials and construction methods such as ferro-cement and glass lenses in a way the English historian of modern architecture Kenneth Frampton characterized recently as a technological triumph: "Confronted by this translucent roof today, one senses that one is looking at a lost art, for this thin-shell combination of ferro-cement and glass lenses, set at close centers, is a technique we now could no longer master or maintain."[41]

Tyl's Bondy Passage, which is the most accomplished of Prague's arcades, used concrete and glass lenses not only for its vaulted ceilings but also for galleries around the arcade. It is not surprising that several photographers made it a subject of their pictures, including Josef Sudek, Jiří Lehovec, and Miroslav Dvořák, as its application of glass lenses created interesting optical effects. Each of the three photographers interpreted the arcade in a different way: while Sudek's pictures convey the arcade's expansive space and atmosphere, Lehovec and Dvořák's opted for more detailed explorations of optical effects which can be seen as related to the voyeuristic roots of the arcades.

The status tradition of innovation and modernization associated with the arcade continued in another new building type born out of the rise of consumption—the department store—which emerged in mid-19th century Paris. As a result, the department store has been called the "heir to modernizing tradition pioneered in the passages"[42] and achieved a highly iconic status not only in the history of architecture but also in such recent disciplines as the cultural history of consumption, gender studies, and in the studies of modernity in general.[43]

This status should not come as a surprise, considering the central role of consumption in modern society and the close association between the department store and the advent of

Josef Voříšek

Steel and Glass (Baťa Department Store, Prague-New Town), c. 1932
Baťa Construction Office (Jindřich Svoboda, Consultant Ludvík Kysela), 1927–29
Private collection

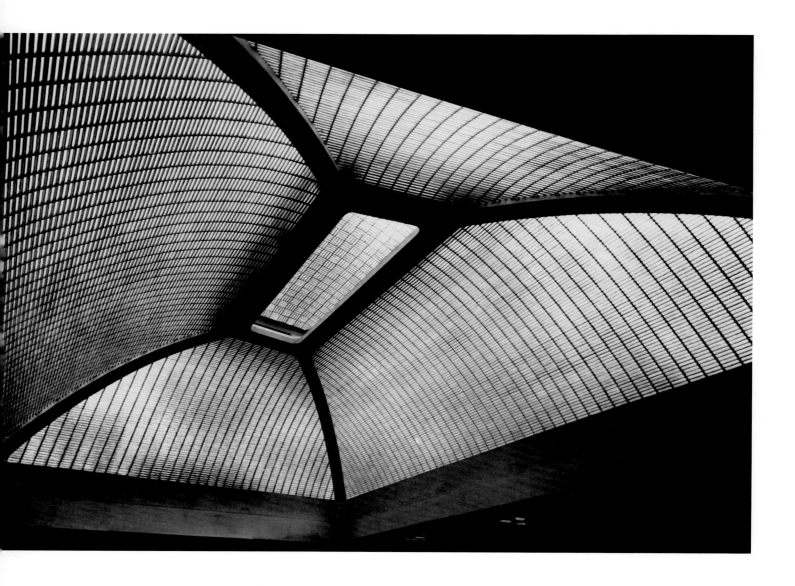

modern consumer society. Until the 19th century, shopping was limited and not considered social activity as goods were procured primarily through barter or self-production.[44] The rise of consumption was closely linked to the emergence of the department store which was aptly called the "cathedral of commerce" by the French writer Émile Zola, who was perhaps the first student of this building type and its cultural, economic, and social ramifications.[45]

    The most distinct characteristic of the department store was its high visibility. Its purpose was to attract attention and curiosity, and ultimately stimulate the desire of the public to buy. This motivation inspired technological innovation, applications of new technologies such as the use of new materials and construction methods for which the department store became known. This made possible such innovations as the creation of plate-glass windows as well as large internal spaces, including top-lit atriums and galleries. Thus the emergence and development of these new forms in the history of architecture was connected to other innovations ushered in by the department store, including modernization in retail distribution, organization of sales, as well as in the organization of urban space.[46]

Photographer unknown
Broadway Passage, Prague-New Town,
c. 1938
Architects Bohumír Kozák and Antonín
Černý, 1936–38
Private collection

Josef Sudek ▶
Bondy Passage (Černá růže), Prague-New
Town, c. 1933
Architect Oldřich Tyl, 1929–33
Private collection

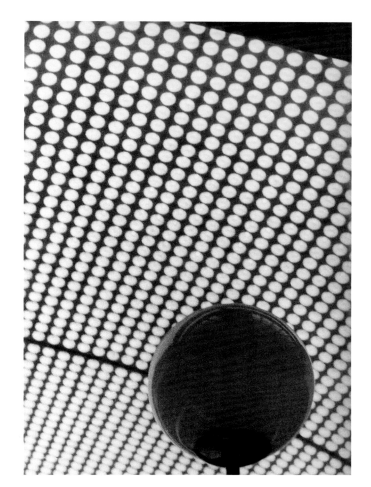

Josef Sudek
Bondy Passage (Černá růže), Prague-New Town, c. 1933
Architect Oldřich Tyl, 1929–33
Private collection

Jiří Lehovec
Ceiling of the Černá Růže Passage (Bondy Passage, Prague-New Town), 1935
Architect Oldřich Tyl, 1929–33
Moravian Gallery, Brno

Miroslav Dvořák
View from Below (Bondy Passage, Prague-New Town), c. 1937
Architect Oldřich Tyl, 1929–33
In: *Fotografie 4,* no.10, Praha: 1937, p. 160

This larger framework of the cultural, economic, and social environment can contribute to a more nuanced reading of architectural discourse as well as to interpretations of individual architectural photographs. The two photographic pictures of the Baťa Department Store in Prague (1927–29) designed by Jindřich Svoboda of the Baťa Building Department (with Ludvík Kysela as a consultant) reflect two different aspects of the building's most prominent feature, a glass and steel façade in the form of a curtain-wall construction, which represented the cutting edge in new construction technologies and new building materials of the day. As its title *Steel and Glass* [Ocel a sklo] indicates, the photograph of the Baťa store (c. 1932) by Josef Voříšek makes exactly this point. Taken from below, it highlights new materials and their physical qualities, notably their optical characteristics such as reflectivity and transparency and their changing relationship in the sun and shade. The use of new materials increased visibility and made the most of display without and within, goals which characterized the department store from its beginnings and informed its use and development of iron frame (and later steel frame) technology and plate-glass windows.[47] The other picture of the Baťa department store, which

Photographer unknown

Wenceslaus Passage, Prague-New Town, c. 1938

Architect E. Kosiner, 1938

Private collection

Josef Sudek ▷

Passage, Legiobanka, Prague-New Town, c. 1939

Architect František Marek, 1937-39

Private collection

was taken by a Centropress Agency photographer, depicts it as a radiant and highly visible structure in the night. Illuminated from the inside, the whole building is transformed into an advertising medium. The external image of the building is used to communicate (more precisely to promote) products as well as corporate identity. In Czechoslovakia, Baťa pioneered this use of architecture, but for all its novelty, this trend was already present in the heroic period of the department store in the West, especially in France in the period between 1880 and 1914.[48] Other social and economic phenomena that accompanied the expansion of the Baťa company, including the social and political debates about organized capitalism and its negative impact on shopkeepers and craftsmen, can be also found in the West in the late 19th and early 20th century. Like the first department stores owners, such as the Boucicauts at Bon Marché in Paris in the last decades of the 19th century, Baťa introduced modernization in the style of management and rationalization in organizing the retail workforce as well as various elements of welfare for its employees, including canteens, medical services, pensions, as well as leisure activities.[49]

But the Baťa company was also a pioneer in new trends that characterized the evolution of the department store in interwar Europe. The main trend was then the impact of American-style retailing on European store owners and managers who traveled to the U.S. to learn new management ideas. Baťa went to the U.S. right after the war, although he was familiar with the American economy from his earlier visit in 1904. The Baťa chain stores became known for their pricing which was standardized into conventionally rising levels, eliminating expenses for ticketing operations. Known in Europe under the name *prix uniques*, this retailing innovation was imported from the U.S. where it was called the 'five and ten stores'.[50] Unlike the classic

Photographer unknown
Baťa Department Store, Zlín, 1930s
Architect František Lydie Gahura, 1929
Private collection

department store, *prix uniques*, of which the Baťa stores were a prime example, entered new lower-middle and working class markets, focusing on standardized objects of mass consumption. These characteristics were most developed in the Baťa Department Store in Zlín (1929), the largest store in Czechoslovakia. Its prominent location at Zlín's main public space called Náměstí práce [Work Square] heralded the post-war evolution of consumerism and the growing impact of consumption on social, economic, and cultural developments.

In 1937 the architects Josef Kittrich and Josef Hrubý designed the Bílá Labuť Department Store in Prague (1937–39) which utilized the most recent technologies, including the most advanced systems for heating, artificial ventilation, air-conditioning, and lighting. It was equipped with lifts, paternosters, conveyors and pneumatic post, and its street façade consisted of a 30 by 20 meter Thermolux glass wall. Supported by a steel skeleton, the glass façade provided shop floors with daylight and in the night it was illuminated with artificial light.[51]

Together with Jan Gillar, who designed the department store's interior, the architects were proponents of radical functionalism who saw architecture as science, not art. As members of the Left Front and the Socialist Union of Architects professing social radicalism, their commitment to the building type which was seen as a symbol of organized capitalism might seem to be a glaring contradiction. However, the ideas of rationalization and scientific approach which they advocated in architecture were associated with the department store from its beginnings in the 19th century—a fact that becomes obvious by realizing how many of the features presented by the architects as novelties, including lifts, conveyors, pneumatic post, and a special system for lighting and advertising, were already present in the 19th-century department store.[52]

industrial
architecture

Structural engineering left all its means at the disposal of the art of modern building. New structures and materials together with new human tasks and views transformed the historical conception of architecture as a fine art, that is formalized art, into a new program of scientific and industrial architecture.

Karel Teige, "The Architecture of the Industrial Age [Architektura průmyslové doby]," 1925

industrial
architecture

One of the most publicized works of new architecture in Czechoslovakia was the ESSO power plant in Kolín (1929–32) designed by Jaroslav Fragner. In 1932 the leading art magazine *Volné směry* featured Fragner's article on the project illustrated with two full-page photographs of the building by Jaromír Funke and Eugen Wiškovský.[53] Since then, Funke's and Wiškovský's photographs have appeared in two different contexts, notably the history of modern architecture and the history of modern photography, fulfilling different functions: in one case serving as architectural representations, in the other as examples of the photographic image.

However, the two genres were originally closely interconnected: in the 19th century, almost every larger industrial building was the subject of documentary photographs, often made by a leading professional photographer (such as Jindřich Eckert in Prague). Thus the collaboration of distinguished photographers and architects was not unprecedented. What is unusual about the ESSO power plant is that its building was photographed not by one but by several leading photographers: Funke, Wiškovský, Josef Sudek, and Jindřich (Heinrich) Koch. Their pictures provide a rare opportunity to compare individual interpretations of a representative example of the new architecture by different protagonists of modern photography. The pictures by Funke and Wiškovský are very similar as they use the same devices associated with the avant-garde (the term constructivism has also been used in this context), such as geometric forms, diagonal compositions and unusual points of view. Some of their pictures resemble each other so much that they only seem to be variations on the same subject. For instance, Funke's picture of the plant smokestack framed by girders, reproduced in *Volné směry*, was taken from almost the same spot as a picture of the same subject by Wiškovský (not reproduced in *Volné směry*). Nevertheless, although these works share the same subject and point of view, they also differ to some extent: the smokestack is framed by girders in Funke's picture, in Wiškovský's work, the girders overlap it, giving the image a different twist. While Funke built his composition around the smokestack, Wiškovský used the smokestack only as one of several motifs in his composition. As a consequence, Wiškovský's composition is more abstract, Funke's composition more monumental. Tonal values of the two pictures are also different: Wiškovský prefers higher contrast and more detail than Funke.

These characteristics seem to extend to other photographs of the ESSO power plant by the two photographers. Wiškovský's photographs of industrial architecture highlight geometric composition and the texture of photographed objects, while Funke's pictures are more hierarchical—they focus on one object, most often the smokestack, underlining its iconographical connotations. This reading might be supported by the fact that, unlike Wiškovský, Funke was interested in surrealism and at the same time took pictures in the manner of the surrealist genre of unexpected encounters, including pictures of a plant smokestack.[54]

Sudek's and Koch's pictures of the ESSO power plant represent another approach. In comparison to Wiškovský's and Funke's work, they are more objective or, more precisely, object-oriented; for instance they do not use unusual angles or diagonal compositions. Sudek's photographs include the plant's interior and exterior, showing some of the construction features of the building, while Koch's pictures represent larger views of the plant seen from

Jaromír Funke

From the series *New Architecture*
(ESSO Power Plant), Kolín, 1931–32
Architect Jaroslav Fragner, 1929–32
Private collection

Eugen Wiškovský

ESSO Power Plant, Kolín, 1932

Architect Jaroslav Fragner, 1929–32

Private collection

Jaromír Funke

ESSO Power Plant, Kolín, 1931–32

Architect Jaroslav Fragner, 1929–32

Private collection

Jaromír Funke

From the series *New Architecture*
(ESSO Power Plant, Kolín), 1931–32
Architect Jaroslav Fragner, 1929–32
Private collection

Eugen Wiškovský

ESSO Power Plant, Kolín, 1932

Architect Jaroslav Fragner, 1929–32

Private collection

Eugen Wiškovský
ESSO Power Plant, Kolín, 1932
Architect Jaroslav Fragner, 1929–32
Private collection

Jindřich (Heinrich) Koch ▸
ESSO Power Plant, Kolín, 1933
Architect Jaroslav Fragner, 1929–32
Private collection

Jindřich (Heinrich) Koch
ESSO Power Plant, Kolín, 1933
Architect Jaroslav Fragner, 1929–32
Private collection

Jindřich (Heinrich) Koch
ESSO Power Plant, Kolín, 1933
Architect Jaroslav Fragner, 1929–32
Private collection

Josef Sudek
ESSO Power Plant, Kolín, 1932
Architect Jaroslav Fragner, 1929–32
Private collection

Josef Sudek
ESSO Power Plant, Kolín, 1932
Architect Jaroslav Fragner, 1929–32
Private collection

Press Photo Agency

Pharmaceutical Plant, Dolní Měcholupy, 1930

Architect Jaroslav Fragner, 1929–30

Private collection

Arno Pařík
Bridge, Kralupy, c. 1927
Architect Jiří Kroha, 1925–27
Private collection

Staša Jílovská
Transformer, c. 1935
Private collection

Josef Sudek ▸
Gasworks (Prague Gasworks in Prague-Michle), c. 1930
Museum of Decorative Arts, Prague

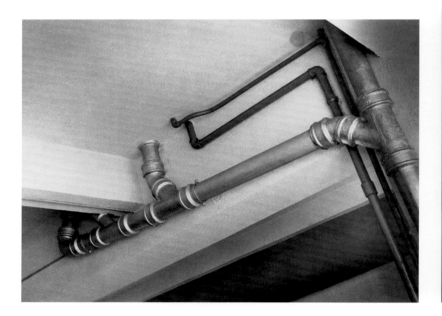

different distances and sides. Both photographers emphasize the technical beauty of their subject, be it the whole building or its individual parts. Although their approaches are similar, a closer examination reveals interesting differences.

In Sudek's work, there are traces of a pictorial "play of lights and shadows," although they might be barely visible. For instance, the picture of a conveyor belt connected to the plant's semi-transparent walls (p.73) cannot possibly be called pictorialist. The graphic depiction of the two objects, the angular steel construction (which supports the conveyor in the foreground) and the white and partly transparent wall, gives them an almost figurative presence, which might have inspired Teige's sexual interpretation of this picture in one of his collages in 1938.[55] However, the picture's contrast between the exterior and the interior of the building, which inspired the collage by Teige, is produced to large extent by light and shadows in the plant's interior seen through the building's glass walls.

Koch harnessed light for a different aesthetic game: he was not interested in the activity of light and shadows but in reflected light that made the photographed object shine, and thus revealed its unique splendor. The power plant, a building type we today associate with pollution, is depicted here not only as pure and clean, but also as radiating light—that is, almost in religious terms.

Jaromír Funke

From the series New Architecture (Masaryk Student Dormitories, Brno-Veveří), 1930
Architect Bohuslav Fuchs, 1929–30
Brno City Museum, Architecture Collection

Studio de Sandalo (?)

Untitled (Boiler, Avia Cinema, Brno-Černovice), c. 1929
Private collection

Studio de Sandalo

Municipal Baths (Distribution of Hot Water),
Brno-Zábrdovice, c. 1931

Architect Bohuslav Fuchs, 1929–31

Brno City Museum, Architecture Collection

The work of the four photographers demonstrates that even within the new photography movement an identical subject can be interpreted in diverse ways by spinning its meaning in different directions. What the works of the four photographers share is their inclination to celebrate industrial objects, a tendency that is usually associated with the machine aesthetic of the 1920s, but which also had its origins in 19th-century documentary photography.[56] Avant-garde architects and photographers believed that photography was a messenger of the new beauty of the machine and technology. Thus Wiškovský, Funke, Sudek, Sandalo, and other photographers took pictures not only of industrial buildings but also various industrial forms and systems that were part of any building. Funke's photographs of plumbing from the Masaryk student dormitories in Brno designed by Bohuslav Fuchs, Sandalo's pictures of the water heating and circulation system at the municipal baths in Brno-Zábrdovice, the picture of a boiler from the Avia Cinema in Brno, and Sudek's photographs of the Prague Gasworks showed "how under the sober, matter-of-fact surface of the modern building is hidden a very complex organism," to use the phrase from the catalogue *Exhibition In Praise of the New Architecture.*[57] They revealed the hidden infrastructures as beautiful in their own right, anticipating the infrastructural rhetoric in the architecture of the 1960s and 1970s manifested in the Centre Georges Pompidou (1972–77) by Renzo Piano and Richard Rogers or in the work of the English Archigram Group.

z l í n

Karel Ludwig
Baťa Administrative Building, Zlín, c. 1939
Architect Vladimír Karfík, 1937–38
Private collection

Baťa's factory town in Zlín is an exceptionally sophisticated example of the development planning of an industrial establishment. Its founder devoted as much attention to construction enterprise as he did to all activities and circumstances associated with the growth of the factory.

Otakar Štepánek, *The Architecture of Industrial Buildings* [Architektura průmyslových staveb], 1936

In 1935 Jan A. Baťa commissioned the Swiss architect Le Corbusier to design a master plan for the development zone along the Dřevnice River from Zlín to Otrokovice that would accommodate future urban growth. Le Corbusier's plan for Baťa was not realized, but Baťa's commission as well as Le Corbusier's comments indicate that Zlín was a unique experiment in wedding modern architecture and industrial production.

After his visit to Zlín in 1935, Le Corbusier sent a letter addressed to "Mr. J. A. Baťa and his Co-workers" in which he wrote about his impressions of the town. He approved of the fact that the inner walls of factory buildings and schools in Zlín were whitewashed, as well as "the standardization of all supporting parts of buildings." But he was most impressed by "the intensive use of machines, partly, the endeavor thereby to deliver people from toil and to use the freedom thus gained for higher aims such as education, progress, and uplifting the masses." He closed his letter with high praise of Zlín as a model city contrasted with the traditional cultural center of Europe—Paris: "Zlín is, when everything is told, one of the hot places of the new world: there is life in it! In Paris I have not met anything like Zlín; things in Paris are such that we are asking whether we have not lulled ourselves to sleep."[58]

The founder of the Baťa Shoe Works, Tomáš Baťa, started the company from scratch with his brother in 1894 and developed it into an international empire in three decades. Building his factories not only throughout Europe but also in Asia, Africa, and America and printing advertising brochures in 26 languages, including Hindu and Chinese, his corporation has to be regarded as a harbinger of globalization.[59] Baťa was keen on the role of modern architecture, choosing Jan Kotěra, the foremost Czech architect of the period, to design his house in 1911 and a workers settlement in 1918. More importantly, Baťa recognized the significance of standardization together with modern construction methods and materials such as steel, reinforced concrete, and glass.[60]

Le Corbusier compared Zlín to an "American anthill" (his letter was published in a publication which was characteristically titled *Zlín: The Town of Activity* and produced by the Baťa Shoe Works Publishing Department), hinting at obvious parallels between Baťa's corporate town and the American way of life.[61] Baťa visited the U.S. in 1904–05 and 1919 and adopted a number of particular ideas as well as general ones that characterized American life, including the American work ethic and pragmatism. He found inspiration in the work of Henry Ford while experimenting with new forms of management and marketing. Baťa's embrace of the American industrial model was manifested in the reinforced concrete frame chosen by Baťa and his engineers as a universal construction module for both industrial and public buildings as its form and size of 7 by 7 meters were appropriated from American factory plans Tomáš Baťa owned.

This standardization endowed Zlín architecture with its specific character described aptly by the Zlín city architect František Lydie Gahura when he emphasized a new conception of industrial city intended "to grow organically out of forms of industrial architecture." According to Gahura, "the main influence on Zlín's appearance stems from the factory building itself [as] it is repeated in numerous variations in all structures, serving public purposes, schools, dormitories, the Společenský Dům Hotel [Community House], the Social Welfare Institute, etc."

Photographer unknown

Zlín, Shoes for the Whole World, 1930s

Private collection

These variations were based on a structural, industrial standard, notably "structural unit in rein-forced concrete or steel skeleton construction forming square bays of 7 by 7 meters."[62]

Standardization on the scale advanced by Baťa was possible only in a town that was practically owned by one corporation. In the 1920s and 1930s, Zlín was a rare (although not unique) example of an urban project that, in its whole as well as in its individual buildings, rep-resented a corporate identity. This concept of urban planning was rooted in the late 19th-cen-tury reform movement which inspired the rise of factory towns in the U.S., Germany, and other countries. The movement's seminal book *Garden Cities of Tomorrow* by Ebenezer Howard (published by Sonnenschein & Co. in London in 1902) appeared in Czech translation under the title *Zahradní města budoucnosti* in Prague in 1924.[63] While early industrial structures often adopted historical forms of other building types, the Zlín builders employed a construction form emblematic of industrial architecture. This approach not only reflected their effort to achieve the most functional and cost-effective solution but also their aspiration to contribute to the "new conception of life and work of an industrial city."[64] According to Jiří Voženílek, one of the Baťa architects, "Zlín was an outstanding environment because everything that was being done, every work, made sense."[65]

Zlín was not only a shoe town, as it was depicted in postcards that showed a cut-out view of the town in the form of a shoe, but a symbol of a new world that provided seemingly endless possibilities identified with modern technology, industrial production, and corporate

Photographer unknown
View from the Baťa Administrative Building,
Zlín, c. 1940
Private collection

Photographer unknown
View from the Baťa Administrative Building,
Zlín, c. 1940
Private collection

Photographer unknown
*Big Cinema and the Společenský Dům
Hotel, Zlín,* 1930s
Architects František Lydie Gahura (cinema),
1931–32; Vladimír Karfík (hotel), 1932–33
Private collection

Photographer unknown
*Big Cinema and the Společenský Dům
Hotel, Zlín,* 1930s
Architects František Lydie Gahura (cinema),
1931–32; Vladimír Karfík (hotel), 1932–33
Private collection

Photographer unknown

Café Terrace, Společenský Dům Hotel,
Zlín, 1930s
Architect Vladimír Karfík, 1932–33
Private collection

Photographer unknown

Společenský Dům Hotel, Zlín, 1930s
Architect Vladimír Karfík, 1932–33
Private collection

Photographer unknown
Společenský Dům Hotel, Otrokovice, 1930s
Architect Vladimír Karfík, 1933–36
Private collection

Photographer unknown
Společenský Dům Hotel, Otrokovice, 1930s
Architect Vladimír Karfík, 1933–36
Private collection

organization. This vision is exemplified by photomontage postcards of Zlín that presented a composite image of the town's most prominent buildings with attributes of technological progress such as a racing car, airplane, and radio transmitter, as well as portraits of Tomáš and Jan Baťa.

Built in a short period of about one decade, Zlín's dominant structures such as the Společenský Dům Hotel (1932–33), the Baťa Department Store (1929), the Big Cinema (1931–32), the Baťa Administrative Building (1937–38), the Baťa schools (1927–28), and the Baťa Memorial (1932–33), which were located around or in the vicinity of so-called Náměstí práce [Work Square], represented technological achievements and innovations for their respective building types. The Baťa administrative building, for example, was the first administrative building in Czechoslovakia equipped with large office spaces: on each of the seventeen stories there were 150–200 workers. The building included amenities such as an office for Jan Baťa, located in a 6 by 6 meter air-conditioned elevator with running water, communications system, and an automatic door which, as its architect Vladimír Karfík noted, enabled Baťa to watch his employees on every floor.[66]

Zlín's Big Cinema (1931–32), designed by F. L. Gahura in collaboration with B. Martinec and Vtelenský, the engineer of the Baťa Building Department, was the largest in Czechoslovakia, with 2,500 seats and a special steel construction of innovative design. Baťa recognized in cinema a powerful medium of marketing, advertising and education, and for this purpose, he also built a modern film studio (1935–36) which made films that advertised company products as well as educational films for the Baťa schools and workers. Baťa planned to produce 16 mm

Studio de Sandalo
Tomáš Baťa Memorial, Zlín, 1930s
Architect František Lydie Gahura, 1932–33
Private collection

Photographer unknown ▸
Tomáš Baťa Memorial, Zlín, 1930s
Architect František Lydie Gahura, 1932–33
Private collection

film projectors and equip schools as well as his stores with them to enhance shopping experience and advance marketing opportunities, anticipating today's use of video for the same purpose.[67]

Several of Zlín's buildings, the Baťa Department Store (1929), the Společenský Dům Hotel (1932–33), and the Baťa Administrative Building (1937–38) were also the largest or tallest structures of their respective building types in Czechoslovakia. The Společenský Dům Hotel [Community House], which contained several restaurants, cafés, conference rooms, including a rooftop restaurant, was the first hotel skyscraper in Czechoslovakia. The Baťa Memorial used the same construction system of a reinforced concrete frame, but its walls were completely replaced with glass, creating a glass box, which was intended as an entry to the Baťa Learning Institutes. Zlín's educational system, boasting new schools, dormitories, and research institutes built in a park environment, represented a new approach to research and education, which was understood as a prerequisite for industrial growth and as a key element of modern life. According to Karfík, Le Corbusier admired Baťa's education system and methods, stating that in France "we do not know such active learning methods yet."[68]

As Le Corbusier's visit indicates, housing and urban planning were other important fields to which the Zlín architects made significant contributions. The emphasis on free-standing structures in Zlín corresponded with the urbanist concepts of the modern movement which rejected the traditional street grid in favor of structures opened to sun and air. However, Zlín's builders had a vision of urban life that was very different from those pursued by proponents of the International Style. In the introduction to the three-volume book *The Ideal Industrial City of the Future*, which was prepared for publication by the Baťa Building Department in 1937 (but was never printed), Jan Baťa argued that "housing in apartment buildings corrupts morals and one's physical and psychical composure." According to Baťa "the principle is that workers' families should live in single houses with a garden, not in row and apartment buildings or even in 'barracks'."[69]

Hence it is not surprising that Le Corbusier's utopian plan for Zlín, which did not pay much attention to local social and historical elements, was not approved by Baťa.[70] Other avant-garde architects did not fare better in Zlín.[71] And yet Baťa's architects were successfully able to exploit key modern concepts such as standardization,[72] and anticipate some of the future developments in 20th-century architecture, including the growing mobility of the population and the import of modern communication in urban planning. For instance, F. L. Gahura made conjectures on urbanism and housing of the future which were more accurate than predictions by many avant-garde theorists and critics: "Man looking for a place for dwelling will not be dependent on the city grid in today's sense. He will find a place in mountains, forests, on the bank of a river or by a lake, on a vast plane, not dependent on the electric grid and canalization. Distance will become meaningless. He will access thermal and light energy by means of an antenna from the air, by means of mirrors or mirror accumulators of the sun's rays. [...] The housekeeper will order household items by means of wireless telephone and improved department store services."[73]

However, Gahura also cautioned that a "solution of the zoning and building problems is only a small part in the organism of the age, and that this part should be sought not in the roots but in the branches of history."[74] This openness and pragmatism contrasted with the utopian and teleological impulse of the avant-garde. On the other hand, Baťa, who organized celebrations of the 1st of May for his workers, made use of utopianism as a powerful management tool, as his following observation demonstrates: "The bigger, and the more utopian the plan seems to people while they witness how it materializes with every day, the bigger is their effort, the stronger is their trust and faithfulness."[75]

cinematic and
kinetic themes

Screen canvas is the only picture canvas that is worth looking at.

**Jaromír Krejcar, "The Path to Modern Architecture [Cesta
k moderní architektuře]," 1925**

cinematic and
kinetic themes

"Only film can make the new architecture intelligible," observed the Swiss architectural historian and critic Siegfried Giedion in 1928, anticipating the present growing employment of multimedia technologies in design and presentation processes.[76] In the 1920s, artists and critics often voiced their admiration for cinema as a new art form, recognizing its import for traditional media. These statements not only documented cinema's impact on individual art forms, including architecture, but also manifested the beginnings of the reflection on media relationships and exchanges as well as on the development of other new media in the future. For instance, when Le Corbusier stated that the only contemporary art forms were architecture and cinema, he was referring to the parallels between the two media, such as the use of modern technology, their collaborative nature and the necessity of team work, and, most importantly, their impact on popular imagination.[77]

Cinema became the 20th-century paradigm for other media because of its popularity and technological innovation. It demonstrated a radically new method of storytelling—a new way of constructing space and time that corresponded with the modern experience of mobility, dislocation, and fragmentation. The impact of the new medium on architecture raises the question of the complex relationship and links between the two practices, which includes such important issues as how the depiction of architecture on the screen changes its perception and representation.[78] Some of these issues were already addressed by the above-mentioned films that documented the construction of the two most significant administrative buildings, the General Insurance Institute and the Prague Electricity Board. Another important question is what this mediation's import was for architectural practice.

The history of the cinema as a building type engages many of these questions. In his recent publication *Cinema Builders* (2001), Edwin Heathcote showed that the cinema is a modern building type that transformed traditional theater structures by rejecting historicism and adopting the language of the new architecture.[79] The history of Czech architecture provides a number of interesting examples of these developments. For instance, in 1924, *Stavba* included the *Design for a Cinema Theater* by Jan Koula which represented an early example of the emerging modern cinema building.[80] Characteristically, some of these cinema buildings were erected at fairgrounds, such as the cinema with café (designed by Emil Králík) at the Regional Fairgrounds in Brno, indicating a connection between the new medium and other forms of spectacle. In other instances, cinema was incorporated into an exhibition building, for example into the Prague Sample Fair Palace, or into multiple-purpose buildings such as the Olympic building in Prague or the Morava building in Brno.[81]

The Avia Cinema by Josef Kranz (1927–29) was one of the most distinct examples of the emerging cinema building whose design celebrated modern life by connecting forms such as cinema and aviation with the new language of architecture. Its façade orchestrates a delicate play of light and shadows on straight and curved surfaces that could recall the contemporary Villa Stein and Villa Savoy by Le Corbusier. A parallel between Kranz and Le Corbusier can also be seen in the attention they paid to photographs of their buildings. Vintage prints from Kranz's estate suggest that the architect was involved not only in editing photographs of his

Studio de Sandalo (?)
Avia Cinema, Brno-Černovice, 1929
Architect Josef Kranz, 1927–29
Private collection

Studio de Sandalo (?)
Avia Cinema, Brno-Černovice, 1929
Architect Josef Kranz, 1927–29
Private collection

Studio de Sandalo (?)
Avia Cinema, Brno-Černovice, 1929
Architect Josef Kranz, 1927–29
Private collection

Studio de Sandalo (?) ▸
Avia Cinema, Brno-Černovice, 1929
Architect Josef Kranz, 1927–29
Private collection

Studio de Sandalo (?) ▸
Avia Cinema, Brno-Černovice, 1929
Architect Josef Kranz, 1927–29
Private collection

work by using such devices as cropping and retouching, but most probably also in suggesting specific views and lighting for individual shots. The architect's involvement is most visible in his use of a special retouching technique that consisted of a layer of varnish that enabled architects to control tonal values in the photographic representation of their buildings.

A series of pictures of the Avia Cinema provides an almost cinematic representation of the building that evokes movement through the space by sequencing individual architectural themes (such as a staircase, balcony, signage, etc.) as well as by exploiting contrasts of light and shadow that invoke the very medium of cinema. Another effective element of the series is the dichotomy of exterior and interior, amplified by the contrast between daylight and artificial light, light and darkness.

The screen projection defines the cinema as a medium of a collective spectacle whose function is to provide temporary mental release from reality into another realm. It replaced the traditional form of spectacle, the theater, with a new kind of entertainment characterized by its mass effect, which made the cinema building an urban attraction. The replacement of the theater with the cinema is most visible in new urban developments such as Zlín, where the new building type took center stage in public space. In 1932, there were two movie theaters: one was for silent movies, the other for sound films, each with five screenings per day. Like

Photographer unknown

Big Cinema, Zlín, 1930s
Architect František Lydie Gahura, 1931–32
Private collection

Studio de Sandalo

Big Cinema, Zlín, c. 1932

Architect František Lydie Gahura, 1931–32

Private collection

the Baťa Department Store, the new Big Cinema with a capacity for 2,500 people was built at the Náměstí práce [Work Square], prefiguring elements of postindustrial society in which shopping and entertainment would become closely interconnected. This linkage was most evident in Baťa's film productions that included innovative advertising and educational films. The Baťa Works was most probably the only industrial enterprise in the world that built its own film studios to produce educational films as well as commercials that advertised its products.[82]

The advent of sound marked another stage in the evolution of the cinema in which the new building type takes the place occupied by the theater in the 19th century. Sound design then became an important field, which led to collaborations between acoustic experts and sound artists with architects, such as the architect/painter/sound artist Arne Hošek and the architect Čestmír Šlapeta who redesigned the Alfa Cinema in Ostrava (1938).[83]

Another interesting development that showed the impact of cinema on theater consisted of attempts to combine the two arts by creating new multimedia forms. This tendency was represented by the avant-garde theater of Emil F. Burian which developed a multimedia form called Theatergraph, integrating, as the term itself indicates, elements of theater and cinema.[84] Besides the use of the film projection in its dramatic productions, the E.F. Burian Theater organized exhibitions of avant-garde visual art, including a festival of avant-garde film.[85]

Studio de Sandalo

Vlasta Burian Theatre, Prague-New Town, c. 1930
Architect Josef Karel Říha, 1928–30
Private collection

Photographer unknown

Alfa Cinema, Ostrava, c. 1938
Architects Lubomír Šlapeta,1933, and
Čestmír Šlapeta and Arne Hošek, 1938
Vladimír Šlapeta

Vilém Ströminger
A-B Film Studios, Prague-Barrandov, c.1934
Architect Max Urban, 1931–34
Private collection

Photographer unknown

A-B Film Studios, Prague-Barrandov, 1937
Architect Max Urban, 1931–34
Private collection

Photographer unknown
Light Kinetic Sculpture by Zdeněk Pešánek,
Edison Transformer Station, Prague-New
Town, 1930
Private collection

Otakar Vávra and František Pilát
Light Penetrates the Darkness, 1930
35 mm film frame enlargements
Private collection

The growing demand for local film productions in Czechoslovakia in the 1920s resulted in the construction of modern film studios in Prague and Zlín in the 1930s. Thus the increasing consumption of the new medium and the building type associated with it, the cinema, necessitated the rise of another new type, the film studio. Serving production needs of a new kind of industry, the film studio represented a new example of industrial architecture aptly called the 'dream factory'. The fact that the modern film studios in Prague were designed by the architect Max Urban, who was a pioneer filmmaker and the founder of ASUM, one of the first Czech film companies in the early 1910s, is one of numerous examples of how architecture and cinema intersected.[86] The studios were built by the A-B Company in a suburb of Prague called Barrandov (1931–34) which became synonymous with Czech feature films in the way American cinema was identified with Hollywood. The photograph of the A-B Film Studios by Vilém Ströminger, a professional portrait photographer who took numerous pictures of Czech movie stars, reflects these sentiments. His picture depicts the studio building with its *court d'honneur* as if it were a portrait of a glamorous star, as a modern castle shining on the hill—a true dream factory.

Cinema and architecture also intersect in art directing, a specialized discipline deserving separate study in relation to modern architecture. Bedřich Feuerstein's design for the film *Before the Finals* (1932), the avant-garde writer Vladislav Vančura's debut made in collaboration with Svatopluk Innemann, represents an emblematic work in this field.

Light and film projections were other important architectural elements in the 1920s and 1930s. Architects followed the example of theater directors and stage designers who often used these devices and their kinetic effects. This effort is very visible in the work of the Russian constructivists, for instance in the *Design for Pravda Tower Building* by Aleksandr, Leonid, and Viktor Vesnin (1924). It was also present in the work of Czech architects such as Zdeněk Pešánek, who included light and film projections in his multimedia designs for the *Monument to Fallen Pilots* (1924–29). The motif of light and film projections together with the theme of flight also appeared in the work of Jaromír Krejcar, notably in his *Design for the Czechoslovak Pavilion in Paris* (1936), which linked it with the theme of flight, and in the work of Le Corbusier, for instance, in his *Design for the Baťa Pavilion in Paris* (1936).[87]

Zdeněk Pešánek made light and movement the primary medium of his art in the 1920s and 1930s, becoming one of the pioneers of kinetic art. He was also the first artist/architect to introduce kinetic elements into architecture by means of public kinetic sculptures. In 1930 he created a light kinetic sculpture for the Edison Transformer Station in Prague, which consisted of compositional elements such as a circle, sphere, vertical and horizontal motifs. The sculpture projected a colored light show which was programmed on perforated tape.[88] There was a specific affinity between Pešánek's light kinetic sculptures and cinema, since in both cases, light and movement were the principal elements. Pešánek exploited this affinity by collaborating on the film *Light Penetrates the Darkness* (1930) by the avant-garde filmmakers Otakar Vávra and František Pilát, which was devoted to his kinetic sculpture for the Edison Transformer Station and its theme of electricity. Its authors explored and elaborated the sculpture's kinetic elements by cinematic means, linking the kinetic and the cinematic together in the spirit of Siegfried Giedion's statement "Only film can make the new architecture intelligible."[89]

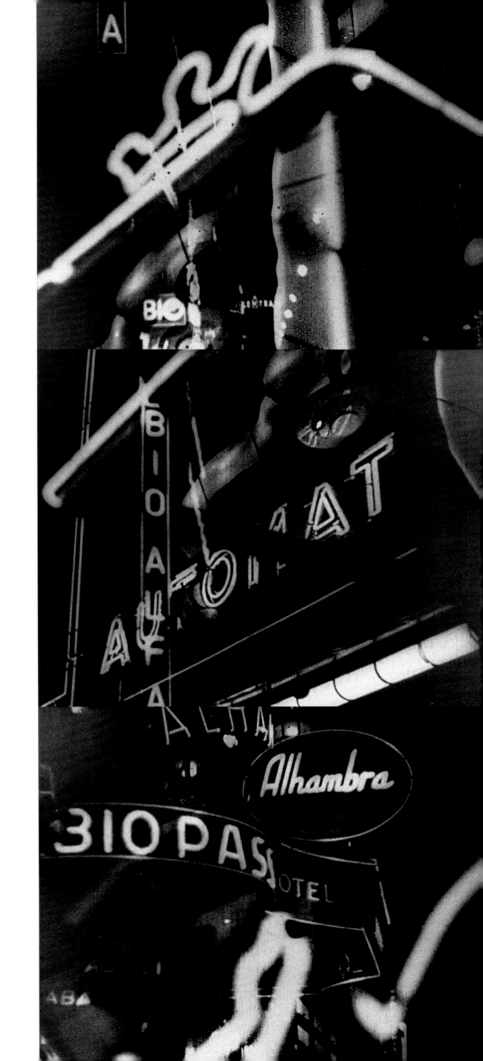

Svatopluk Innemann
Prague Shining in Lights, 1928
35 mm film frame enlargements
Private collection

aviation
references

The shape of the airplane is inseparable from its construction. It is absolutely devoid of any decorativism since it follows clear goals [...]

Vilém Santholzer, "The Shape of the Airplane [Plastika Aeroplanu]," 1925

Photographer unknown
Airplane Engine, 1920s
Private collection

a v i a t i o n
r e f e r e n c e s

The airplane occupied a prominent position among forms of modern life associated with new architecture as the quoted anthology *Life; Anthology of the New Beauty* demonstrated. Besides two illustrations of airplanes, the publication included an aerial view of lower Manhattan as well as a photograph of a flying plane surrounded by New York skyscrapers, a motif explored a few years later by Jaroslav Rössler in one of his picture poems. The airplane as well as other popular subjects associated with the theme of aviation, such as the airplane engine and aerial photographs, were often reproduced in architectural magazines and books so that it comes as no surprise that they eventually appeared as prominent motifs in architectural projects and realizations.

In this respect, the project of a house-airplane by Otto Klein (1930–31) is most explicit. Aeronautic inspiration is also manifested in the Hain House in Prague-Vysočany (1932–33), built for an aviation engineer and designed by Ladislav Žák, especially in the cantilevered terrace and the cantilevered crow's nest. However, aeronautical motifs most often appeared in exhibition pavilions.[90] For instance, the Exhibition of Czechoslovak Architecture and Design in Stockholm (1931) designed by Ladislav Sutnar and Bohuslav Fuchs incorporated a series of aerial photographs of urban structures in Czechoslovakia, juxtaposed with two airplanes suspended from the ceiling. In his Czechoslovak Pavilion at the World Exhibition in Paris in 1937, Jaromír Krejcar employed aviation references such as an observation tower outside and an airplane suspended from a Thermolux glass ceiling inside.

In this context, the Tomáš Baťa Memorial in Zlín (1932–33) designed by František Lydie Gahura represented an interesting case, since the building combined two functions/building types: the memorial and the exhibition pavilion. As a consequence, the exhibited plane, which belonged to the founder of the Baťa Shoe Company, Tomáš Baťa, who died in a plane crash in 1932, functioned as a symbol of technological progress on one hand and as a commemoration of its owner and his tragic death on the other. Designed as a glass box, the building with this double function could have existed perhaps only in Zlín, the corporate headquarters of a global company and a new industrial center built by its founder from scratch (see the chapter on Zlín in this book).

The impact of aviation on the popular imagination was manifested in the spread of names such as Avion and Avia that were used for such diverse building types as hotels and cinemas, as two prominent examples of the new architecture in Brno indicate, the Avion Hotel (1926–27) by Bohuslav Fuchs and the Avia Cinema by Josef Kranz. This popularity was fostered by the spread of aviation and the growth of an aeronautic industry reflected by Tomáš Baťa's own strong enthusiasm for aviation. Baťa built a new airport for Zlín (1932) at Otrokovice where the Baťa Works started a production line of light airplanes a few years later.[91] The emerging network of airports produced another new building type or types—the airport building and the hangar—which were understood as an expression of modern life paradigmatic of the new architecture.[92]

The comparison of two examples, the airport building in Prague-Ruzyně (1932–34) by Adolf Benš with the airport building in Marienbad (1927–29), designed by Pavel Janák several

Jaroslav Rössler
Unlife, 1926
Collage
Private collection

Photographer unknown

Czechoslovak Pavilion in Paris, 1937

Architect Jaromír Krejcar, 1936–37

Private collection

Josef Voříšek ▶

Czechoslovak Pavilion in Paris, 1937

Architect Jaromír Krejcar, 1936–37

Private collection

years earlier, demonstrates a rapid evolution of this type. While Janák's building is a relatively simple box, Prague's airport building represents a more complex structure that included almost all components found in contemporary airports. It consists of an entrance hall with a segmentally shaped skylight, a glass flight-control tower with rounded corners and balconies, and two wings, one of which carried a series of antennae on the flat roof. Each section of the building complex thus communicated its function by symbolizing different ways of connecting the building with the skies.

The popularity of aviation was also reflected by the spread of aviation clubs found in a number of cities throughout Czechoslovakia in the 1920s and 1930s. Zlín and Brno, centers of the new architecture, were at the forefront of the movement of amateur aviators. The Baťa company supported this development by establishing a flying school in Zlín.[93] Flying was popular among some artists and photographers. For instance, Josef Voříšek was an airplane designer, and Hugo Táborský, an avant-garde designer and photographer was a member of the Moravia Aviation Club in Brno for which he created a logo and letterhead. He also took

Studio de Sandalo
Tomáš Baťa Memorial, Zlín, c. 1933
Architect František Lydie Gahura, 1932–33
Private collection

Photographer unknown
Tomáš Baťa Memorial, Zlín, 1930s
Architect František Lydie Gahura, 1932–33
Private collection

Photographer unknown ▸
AP 32, 1931
Private collection

an interest in aerial photography, a photographic genre that received a lot of attention in avant-garde and architectural magazines as well as in architectural exhibitions, including the architectural section of the *Exhibition of Contemporary Culture in Czechoslovakia* in Brno (1928), the *Exhibition of Czechoslovak Architecture and Design* in Stockholm (1931), and the *Exhibition of Construction Industry and Housing* in Prague (1932) and Brno (1933).

Aerial views, which were introduced by 19th-century balloonists, pioneers of aerospace exploration, had a revolutionary impact on pictorial representation, including architecture, by subverting established representational conventions based on linear perspective. There was a connection between aerial photography and new pictorial idioms such as impressionism; the impressionist painters, who, for instance, adopted bird's-eye view compositions in some of their works, held their first exhibition at the studio of Nadar, a leading photographer who was also a pioneer balloonist and author of the first aerial photographs. Aerial photographs

Photographer unknown
Untitled (Airport, Prague-Kbely), 1930s
Private collection

Photographer unknown ▸
*Water Tower and Airport Lighthouse,
Prague-Kbely,* c. 1925
Architect Otakar Novotný, 1924
Private collection

were also a source of inspiration for pioneers of abstract painting, including Kazimir Malevich and Robert Delaunay in the 1910s, and continued to provide painters with pictorial solutions through the 1920s.[94] In the second half of the 1920s, the two most prominent Devětsil painters, Jindřich Štyrský and Toyen, developed an abstract style called artificialism which was directly inspired by aerial photographs.[95] Their paintings paralleled the rise of the new photography movement identified with the phrase the "new vision," in which unusual views such as the bird's-eye view played again an instrumental role. Aerial photographs were one of the sources of inspiration for this movement, as demostrated by the exhibition *Film und Foto* in Stuttgart (1929) and the publication *Foto-Auge* by Jan Tschichold and Franz Roh published the same year.[96]

At the same time, the aerial axonometric view became a favored rendering technique in architecture, employed for urban planning as well as for plans of individual buildings. The widespread use of axonometric views, which became a must for design presentations in the 1920s, drew on the popularity of aerial photographs.[97] For instance, Krejcar's *Design for Parliament Building at Letná* (1928) included an aerial axonometric view rendered as if it were seen from an airplane represented by a fragment of its wing in the foreground. These intersections of aviation and the new architecture demonstrate the impact of aviation and aerial photography on architectural imagination while indicating parallel paths of the new architecture and the new photography.[98]

According to the catalogue *In Praise of the New Architecture*, "the primary aim, the driving force of new architecture was the effort to achieve supremacy over heavy matter, a free plan, and the greatest variability possible."[99] The airplane represented not only a symbol of technological progress and the triumph of science and technology, but also the realization of one of the archetypal dreams of mankind—a symbol of freedom that inspired various fields of human activity. As aviators and architects sought to master the forces of gravitation to a greater and greater degree, aerial views and the airplane embodied aspirations of the new architecture and functioned as an attribute and symbol of its bold vision.

o f f i c e
b u i l d i n g s

Jaroslava Hatláková

Modern Architecture (General Pension Institute, Prague-Žižkov), c. 1935

Architects Josef Havlíček and Karel Honzík, 1929–34

Private collection

It was not only about the creation of the high-rise office building type rare in our country, equipped with the latest technical use of land, or high-rise construction. [...] The exterior surface of a building so large, tall and without decoration, an issue which is not so significant in other cases, also had to be solved in a decisive and responsible way.

Jan E. Koula, "The V. P. Ú. Skyscraper in Prague-Žižkov. An Interview with the Designers of the Building Josef Havlíček and Karel Honzík [Mrakodrap V. P. Ú. na Žižkově. Rozmluva s projektanty budovy architekty Josefem Havlíčkem a Karlem Honzíkem]" 1933–34

o f f i c e
b u i l d i n g s

In his introduction to the section devoted to office, retail, and industrial buildings in the exhibition *In Praise of the New Architecture*, the architect Adolf Benš noted that "beneficial circumstances have allowed us to realize several large and technologically distinct buildings of international significance in the field of office/administrative buildings which prove that our work is competent and represents a promising sign for the future."[100] Benš, together with Josef Kříž, was the architect of the Prague Electricity Board building (1927–35), after the General Pension Insurance building the second largest administrative office building in Prague, which explains the sense of achievement and satisfaction conveyed by Benš's statement.

The two buildings became the subject of numerous articles and photographs as well as two monographic publications which focused on the inventive design and new technical features of the two projects.[101] For instance, the publication on the Prague Electricity Board building included detailed technical descriptions of the building and its construction illustrated with high-quality reproductions of approximately 150 photographs. It also included an essay on the social context of the Prague Electricity Board building and of its design which outlined the architects' goals and related them to long-term social and economic transformations. This essay illuminates the architects' intentions and provides a broader historical view whose main point is still valid—notably that the transformation of traditional types and the rise of new building types are grounded in social and economic developments.

Benš and Kříž emphasized "the social significance of the modern office building" and the need to create a perfect building type equipped with many accessible amenities. They saw this need grounded in the changing character of economy, in the fact that "the result of the growth of industrialization and rationalization is that industrial production requires less and less human labor whereas the number of workers associated with administration and distribution is increasing because their agenda is constantly more complex and important." According to the two architects, this was the reason why the significance of the industrial building diminished while that of a new kind of office building grew. The traditional type of the administrative building was replaced with a new type whose purpose was to work, not to represent. Benš and Kříž interpreted this process as democratization and the need for functional standards, drawing from their observation an important conclusion that is still valid today: "The nature of the employee's environment does matter. It impacts his productivity, his psychical and physical health, labor force and with it, all economic and social life."[102]

According to Benš and Kříž, the architect could improve both workers' productivity and the quality of life by creating a new type of office building. Their design reflected this effort in a number of ways, for instance, in its great attention to natural and artificial lighting, temperature and air control (the whole building was equipped with an air-conditioning system, one of the first examples of a fully air-conditioned building in Czechoslovakia), as well as to the capabilities and services which were then not associated with the office building. It included amenities such as a library and reading room, exhibition spaces, classrooms, a cafeteria and kitchen, psychotechnic laboratories, a recreational space, a spa and a health clinic with departments of internal and dental medicine, physical therapy, and radiology.

Štenc Graphic Enterprise
Prague Electricity Board,
Prague-Holešovice, 1935
Architects Adolf Benš and Josef Kříž,
1927–35
Štenc Archive, Prague

Studio de Sandalo
Prague Electricity Board,
Prague-Holešovice, 1935
Architects Adolf Benš and Josef Kříž,
1927–35
Private collection

Studio de Sandalo ▶
Prague Electricity Board,
Prague-Holešovice, 1935
Architects Adolf Benš and Josef Kříž,
1927–35
Private collection

The architects saw themselves as "working on a new form of life, on the character of the new man, who demands space, light, air, and refuses the semi-darkness and closeness of traditional plans, on the character of man who is free, courageous and newly oriented towards society."[103] The Prague Electricity Board building represents a successful materialization of this vision, which is to a various degree present in photographs of the building, depending on the capacity and interests of individual photographers. In this respect, the photographs by Studio de Sandalo communicate the architects' vision most effectively. They show the building's exterior and interiors endowed with light, spaciousness, and purity, expressing a spirit of optimism. It is interesting that these special characteristics are not lost in night views of the building—the whole surface covered with white tiles is lit so that it shines in the darkness and, together with the trajectories of passing car headights, creates the feeling of infinite possibilities of electric energy as well as the excitement of big city life celebrated by the Devětsil artists in the 1920s.[104]

Studio de Sandalo
Prague Electricity Board,
Prague-Holešovice, 1935
Architects Adolf Benš and Josef Kříž,
1927–35
Private collection

ELEKTRICKÉ PODNIKY EP

Studio de Sandalo

Prague Electricity Board,
Prague-Holešovice, 1935
Architects Adolf Benš and Josef Kříž,
1927–35
Private collection

In the quoted essay, Benš and Kříž suggested that the beneficial circumstances for realizations of the new type of the office building consisted in the changing character of the economy reflected by the rising number of white-collar workers. But there were other circumstances as well, including the progressive bent of the young democracy. This characteristic fostered a greater openness to new ideas and created opportunities for young artists and architects as the new state and its institutions recognized in modern architecture a powerful symbol of modernity and progress.

The selection of the design by the Devětsil architects Josef Havlíček and Karel Honzík (then 30 and 29 years old) for the first skyscraper in Prague, the General Pension Institute (VPÚ) building, is a case in point. Based on a cruciform ground-plan, their bold design was derived from the utopian project for the *Ville contemporaine* with three million inhabitants by Le Corbusier (1922), but modified with regards to the character of the site, the slope of the Žižkov quarter.[105] Inspired by Le Corbusier's vision of the future city, the architects conceived the building as an

avatar of the new Prague, as a counterweight raising in the face of the historical city. This symbolic rhetoric manifested itself in the creation of the Club for the New Prague by proponents of the new architecture as a response to the activities of the Club for the Old Prague whose mission was to preserve the historical character of the city.[106]

Unlike most other new office buildings, the VPÚ building's plan was not integrated into the existing city blocks but conceived as a free-standing structure which the architects envisioned to be followed by many other skyscrapers on the Žižkov slope.[107] This major intervention into the cityscape of Prague was thus predicated on the opposition of the old and the new which shaped much of the architectural discourse of the period, and was built into the production as well as the reception of the work of both avant-garde architects and photographers. This opposition was thus an implicit conceptual framework which informed making as well as reading individual architectural photographs.

For instance, the height and the pinwheel plan of the VPÚ building were seen as embodiments of the emerging new world identified with progress and freedom. In her pictures of the structure taken shortly after its completion, Jaroslava Hatláková, a student of Jaromír Funke at the State School of Graphic Arts in Prague, emphasized the building's height by using oblique angles of view and a diagonal composition. Josef Voříšek used the same devices to evoke the mobility of the viewer and the kinetic nature of architectural experience, foregrounding the building's structure.

In the case of most other office buildings, however, the plan had to conform with the existing street grid and was consequently more integrated into the city's organism. Architects reinforced this integration at street level by creating passages with retail spaces that revived

Jaroslava Hatláková

Modern Architecture (General Pension Institute, Prague-Žižkov), c. 1935
Architects Josef Havlíček and Karel Honzík, 1929–34
Private collection

Josef Voříšek

Untitled (General Pension Institute, Prague-Žižkov), c. 1935
Architects Josef Havlíček and Karel Honzík, 1929–34
Private collection

the tradition of the 19th-century arcade. Certain office buildings also served other purposes such as housing and entertainment. Palaces of the first two decades of the 20th century, for instance, the Lucerna Palace in Prague (1907–21) by Václav Havel, were prototypes of multifunctional buildings with cafés and arcades. In the 1920s, this hybrid building type was exemplified by the Olympic Palace in Prague (1923–28) designed by Jaromír Krejcar, a multipurpose building that included a cinema on the underground level, stores on the ground floor, a restaurant with a bar on the first floor, and offices and apartments on its upper floors. The Mines and Steel Company [Báňská a hutní] building in Prague (1928–30) designed by Josef Karel Říha was another new office building which achieved similar integration into city life by incorporating stores and a passage on the ground floor, and the Vlasta Burian Theater in the underground which functioned as a cinema in the afternoon and a theater in the evening.[108]

Arcades and galleries were often lit through glass skylights, an element associated with 19th-century industrial architecture. In their quest to endow new buildings with more light and air, some architects also adopted glass skylights for other spaces in office buildings. New technologies and materials such as glass brick made it possible to develop this theme in an innovative way and Czech architects excelled in this respect.[109] Besides Benš's and Kříž's Electricty Board building, Bohuslav Fuchs's and Arnošt Wiesner's Moravian Bank in Brno (1928–30) and František Marek's Legiobanka building in Prague (1938) represent magnificent examples of the creative usage of these new technologies and materials.

Jaroslav Möller

Báňská a hutní Building, Prague-New Town, c. 1930

Architect Josef Karel Říha, 1928–30

Private collection

Jaroslav Möller
Báňská a hutní Building, Prague-New Town, c. 1930
Architect Josef Karel Říha, 1928–30
Private collection

Photographer unknown

Legiobanka Building, Prague-New Town, c. 1939

Architect František Marek, 1937–39

Private collection

Photographer unknown ▷

Legiobanka Building, Prague-New Town, c. 1939

Architect František Marek, 1937–39

Private collection

s c h o o l s

Studio de Sandalo

Vesna Vocational Schools,
Brno-Stránice, 1930
Bohuslav Fuchs and Josef Polášek, 1929–30
Brno City Museum, Architecture Collection

Indeed the school should be like a semi-sanatorium and should always have terraces. For this reason, it is no longer possible to build schools as row buildings but always as free-standing structures in open lots.

Josef Polášek, "For a Modern School [O moderní školu],"
1931

s c h o o l s

A considerable number of school buildings erected in Czechoslovakia in the 1920s and 1930s were typical examples of the new architecture. The school as a building type exemplified concepts advanced by modern architects such as social function, simplicity, clarity, hygiene, and the access to air and light. The fact that Brno and Zlín, the two cities most often associated with the new architecture in Czechoslovakia, boasted modern school buildings combined with new educational programs is significant in this respect. A case in point is that of the Vesna Women's Vocational Schools and the Eliška Machová Dormitory in Brno designed by Bohuslav Fuchs and Josef Polášek which were widely publicized and hailed as an achievement comparable to the European developments in the Netherlands and Germany.[110]

The Vesna Schools consisted of several buildings that housed departments devoted to all women's professions as well as a teachers' institute and a students' dormitory, together creating a new educational environment. The schools' educational program found its expression in a new concept of the school function described by the architects as follows: "Each classroom in fact constitutes an independent self-contained school, since the space of this unit consists of two parts, one of which is an independent classroom and the other a workshop or examination room. The traditional hallway connecting classrooms is thus eliminated."[111] The architects replaced hallways with balconies that provided access to the open air and light. By using a collapsible wooden partition between the classroom and the workshop, they also provided the option of creating a large room lit by windows on both sides.

The emphasis on function, clarity, simplicity, light, and air is well-depicted by Studio de Sandalo's photographs of the Vesna Schools' interior and exterior. It is also present in the description of the buildings by one of the Vesna teachers: "Sometimes we call it a glass house. And rightly so, since there are only a few walls and the classroom and the workshop are separated from a beautiful landscape only by glass surfaces. But they do not hold us in beautiful captivity. In the summer they are open so that we are in the open air all the time [...] And the balcony provides us with first of all an unrestricted view of a beautiful landscape, a bath of fresh air taken after a strain."[112]

These words were inspired by a new type of school, the so-called open-air school, which came to Czechoslovakia from the Netherlands and Germany. Among its first examples was the kindergarten in Hradec Králové (1926–28) by Josef Gočár; its pictures taken by Josef Sudek show the school's terrace lit by sunshine. The concept of open air informed a number of other new school buildings, including the widely publicized French Schools in Prague (1931–34) by Jan Gillar.

The effort to create a new type of classroom manifested in the Vesna schools reflected new pedagogical ideas that were fostered by the reform movement in education. The relationship between the new school building and new educational concepts was the subject of František Kalivoda's article "Recent School Buildings in Brno" (1937), probably the best outline of theoretical arguments regarding the school as a building type published at the time.[113] Kalivoda emphasized the social responsibility of architects in making the school building serve its purpose well while pointing out that this required meeting specific biological and psychological conditions and needs. According to Kalivoda, the revision of pedagogic methods had to

Jaromír Funke

Masaryk Student Dormitory,
Brno-Veveří, 1930
Architect Bohuslav Fuchs, 1929–30
Moravian Gallery, Brno

140

Centropress

Regional Industrial School,
Mladá Boleslav, c. 1926
Architect Jiří Kroha, 1922–26
Private collection

Centropress

Regional Industrial School,
Mladá Boleslav, c. 1926
Architect Jiří Kroha, 1922–26
Private collection

result in changing the school building type, taking into account the physical and psychical development and care identified with the concept of hygiene. He supported his argument by drawing on the views of the pedagogue Petr Denk, who saw new educational methods leading to new architectural programs. This meant that modern architects had to collaborate with scholars to grasp the "principles of pedagogical processes and establish exactly the function of every individual school space."[114]

Kalivoda characterized the modern school as "a synthesis of modern pedagogical methods, modern building technology, and also hygiene and economy."[115] Consequently, he explored what the architectural implications of the new pedagogy were, and what means the new architecture left at his disposal to meet new educational requirements and needs. Kalivoda's description of the reform movement in education, such as the need to complement theory with practice in different fields of science and technology, the replacement of memorization with practical knowledge and skills, the emphasis on hygiene, physical exercise, light and air, indicates that new architecture and the new pedagogy shared a number of characteristics. It also suggests how much the two tendencies owed to earlier cultural trends, notably to the so-called *Lebens-reform* movement which emerged as a response to the excesses of industrialization in Germany in the late 19th century. It was this movement that popularized the return to nature, for instance physical exercise outdoors, the concept of hygiene, and the worship of the sun.[116]

In fact the rise of vocational schools that connected the classroom with the workshop was closely associated with the *Lebensreform* movement of the late 19th century. Kalivoda

advocated not only the link between the classroom and the workshop but also the association of the classroom with various enterprises such as the factory which could be visited during excursions. He also argued for developing the traditional classroom into different types corresponding with the differentiation of work in modern society and for complementing them with workshops or laboratories. An example of this development can already be found in the Regional Industrial School in Mladá Boleslav (1922–26) designed by Jiří Kroha which included various workshops to educate students in specialization needed in different industries, for instance, in the car industry represented by the Škoda Car Factory, also located in Mladá Boleslav.

The need to differentiate in school buildings between different functions of individual spaces and to use light in the most efficient way encouraged architects to employ the open structure instead of the traditional row building scheme. The new Brno schools, especially those designed by Bohuslav Fuchs, exemplified this development. In 1929 Fuchs also designed the Masaryk Student Dormitory in Brno (1929–30) which shared with the Vesna Schools their open structure as well as a terrace for physical exercise and balconies that connected different rooms.

Numerous photographs of the Masaryk Student Dormitory were taken by different photographers, including Studio de Sandalo and Jaromír Funke, who took a series of pictures of both the buildings' exterior and interior. A brochure on the building was published by Fuchs in 1930 which includes numerous photographs by Funke and Sandalo and represents one of the best examples of this monographic genre.[117] Designed by Emanuel Hrbek, professor at the Brno School of Arts and Crafts, its layout guides the viewer through the building, juxtaposing

Photographer unknown
Kindergarten, Hradec Králové, c. 1929
Josef Gočár, 1926–28
Museum of Decorative Arts, Prague

Josef Sudek ▶
Kindergarten, Hradec Králové, c. 1929
Josef Gočár, 1926–28
Museum of Decorative Arts, Prague

Studio de Sandalo

Elementary School for Boys and Girls,
Brno-Černá Pole, 1931
Architect Mojmír Kyselka, 1930–31
Brno City Museum, Architecture Collection

Studio de Sandalo

Elementary School for Boys and Girls,
Brno-Černá Pole, 1931
Architect Mojmír Kyselka, 1930–31
Brno City Museum, Architecture Collection

different views and angles. While Sandalo's pictures depict individual amenities in a straight-forward manner, Funke's photographs almost exclusively use diagonal compositions that create a dynamic effect. The alternation of different views produces a cinematic feeling amplified by the layout of reproductions in vertical strips.

The emphasis on the functional plan and the effective use of light dovetailed with other concepts associated with the new school building such as cleanliness, purity, hygiene, and simplicity. The complementary character of these concepts and their moral undertone is evident in many writings of the period, including the quoted article on welfare and healthcare in the Teachers' Institute for the Vesna Schools Annual Report for 1931–32: "An easy way of cleaning gives us the option of residing in a permanently clean, dust-free environment. Walls, furniture, windows, everything is smooth without carving and frames, so there are no surfaces where school dust, the greatest bane, can settle."[118] Characteristically, this enthusiastic description of simplicity and purity is followed by passages praising the beneficial effects of air, sunlight, and physical exercise.

A similar moral tone can be detected in the quoted article by Kalivoda and even in the photographs of individual schools that accompanied the article, notably in their emphasis on the large white surfaces of the façades shining in the sunlight. They included the school buildings designed by Josef Polášek (the elementary school in Brno-Obřany, the high school in the Kotlářská Street in Brno-Veveří, and the school in Brno-Královo Pole), Bohuslav Fuchs (the kindergarten in Brno-Husovice), Mojmír Kyselka (the German elementary school in Brno-Černá Pole (1930–31), Florián Kuba

Věra Vaníčková

French Schools, Prague-Dejvice, c. 1935
Architect Jan Gillar, 1931-34
Private collection

Arno Pařík

French Schools, Prague-Dejvice, c. 1935
Architect Jan Gillar, 1931–34
National Technical Museum, Prague

(the elementary school in Brno-Medlánky, the elementary and high school in Brno-Husovice), and Oskar Poříska (the elementary school in Brno-Juliánov, the Tyrš Elementary School in Brno-Židenice, 1928–29).

The most representative in this respect is Studio de Sandalo's photograph of the Elementary School for Boys and Girls in Brno-Černá Pole (1930–31) designed by Mojmír Kyselka (not included in Kalivoda's article) which shows the school's main white façade radiating optimism and self-confidence. Its elegant simplicity, which is based on a symmetric configuration and horizontally-proportioned windows, does not reveal the school's rich program which was inspired by the concept of the open-air school and included such amenities as a garden, playgrounds, and a pool. The photograph evokes Le Corbusier's definition of architecture as a "magnificent play of masses brought together in light" as well as his notion of purism by including such details as the motif of the car and a street lamp whose ornamental design contrasts with the purity of the façade.

Photographs of another school that was widely publicized, notably the French Schools in Prague (1931–34) designed by Jan Gillar, have a similar character. For instance, the photograph by Arno Pařík taken from the street also shows a car in front of the shiny façades. But unlike Sandalo's photograph, it represents a complex configuration of different volumes and levels that reflect the buildings' program consisting of three different schools (the kindergarten, elementary, and high school). Individual buildings are also differentiated in their details, for instance, by the use of different types of windows as if to illustrate the functionalist dictum "form follows function."[119]

sanatoriums
and spas

If we want to present a building representing an image of the new dwelling that we are promoting, it is necessary to point to the spa boarding house in Trenčianske Teplice designed by architect Jaromír Krejcar.

Ladislav Žák, "A Model of the New Dwelling [Předobraz nového bydlení]," 1933–34

s a n a t o r i u m s
a n d   s p a s

Like the café or the school, the sanatorium represents a symbolic institution that reflected social and political developments as well as cultural trends. As Thomas Mann's famous novel *The Magic Mountain* and the great number of new sanatoriums erected in the 1920s and 1930s suggest, this building type became prominent in both popular imagination and the health care system of the time.

The architects František Čermák and Gustav Paul, who specialized in designing health care facilities, recognized the close connection between the boom of sanative buildings and the public's changing view of health care services and hospitals. According to them "the cold and skeptical attitude of the previous generation to sanative public institutions" has transformed itself "into a wholly positive relationship full of understanding and trust" as a result of two developments: "This change of outlook resulted from different social conditions (the downturn of the world labor market and, as a result of it—especially in big cities—the worsened conditions in housing and health care), as well as from the comprehensive improvement of new contemporary hospital facilities and their technical equipment."[120]

This opening paragraph of the article "The Present Construction of Hospitals" published by Čermák and Paul in *Stavba* in 1932 provides a good introduction to the issues associated with the subject. However, both the architectural theory and practice of the period suggests that the change in attitude to health care facilities was much more evident among architects and critics than among the general public. Karel Teige, who more than anyone else promoted the sanatorium as a model building type, grounded this choice in Marxist ideology. In his view, the sanative buildings represented the antithesis of "the holy cow of bourgeois ideology and morality: family and its household," which according to him "forces architecture to stick to outdated forms of dwelling culture." Teige argued that only hospital and social health care buildings could escape the dictate of bourgeois ideology because of the categorical nature of their objective requirements. For this reason, ideology could not intervene in them as crudely as in apartment buildings. For the same reason, Teige claimed that "the most consequential modern building which Central and Western European architecture can present are sanative buildings and some schools." Teige named two works by Johann Duiker, the sanatorium in Hilversum, Netherlands and the open-air school in Amsterdam, Hannes Meyer's workers' school in Bernau near Berlin, and the Altersheim in Frankfurt a.M. by Mart Stam and W. M. Moser. Teige also included three buildings in Czechoslovakia, the municipal pool and spa in Brno-Zábrdovice by Bohuslav Fuchs, the Vesna Schools for Women's Professions by Bohuslav Fuchs and Josef Polášek, and last but not least, Jaromír Krejcar's sanatorium in Trenčianske Teplice."[121]

Teige's argument indicates that it was primarily the avant-garde's sociopolitical views advancing the idea of a new social order and collectivism, notably the belief in the extinction of family and social classes that made it embrace building types such as the sanatorium and the school. As Čermák and Paul suggested in the quoted article, this belief became stronger as a consequence of the Depression, contributing to the political radicalization of avant-garde artists and architects in the 1930s. However, not all the themes associated with these building types had their roots in Marxist radicalism. The themes of light, air, and hygiene that were as,

Photographer unknown

Radun Boarding House, Luhačovice, c. 1927
Architect Bohuslav Fuchs, 1927
Brno City Museum, Architecture Collection

Photographer unknow

Sanatorium, Vráž, 1930s
Architects František Čermák, Gustav Paul,
Antonín Tenzer, 1934–35
Private collection

if not more, prominent for the sanatorium as they were for the school, did not originate in the revolutionary ideology of collectivism but in the reform movement—in the effort to change lifestyle, not social order.[122]

These themes are very much present in pictures of sanatoriums taken by various photographers. For instance, one of the photographs of the boarding house/sanatorium Radun in Luhačovice (1927) designed by Bohuslav Fuchs is taken from a point above the building to show a group of people exercising on one of the building's terraces. The image, complemented by a picture taken from the opposite direction, elicits a feeling of the open air, openness and mobility, amplified by the choice of an unusual camera angle. The photographer thus exploited a device which was then becoming a hallmark of avant-garde photography—oblique perspective—to advance a specific architectural program.

The theme of access to the sun and fresh air is elaborated much more in the Machnáč Sanatorium in Trenčianske Teplice (1929–32) by Jaromír Krejcar. The building was equipped with open terraces (one for men and one for women) with built-in sand pits, showers, and pergolas (which were called sun and sand baths) as well as with a covered terrace and roof garden. Moreover, each patient's room had its own small balcony. Krejcar's interpretation of the two themes, the terrace and the balcony, was informed by the work of two leading architects of the time, Le Corbusier and Walter Gropius, notably by the roof gardens and terraces of Le Corbusier's villas of the 1920s and by the Eastern wing of Walter Gropius's Bauhaus which had an almost identical design. In his monograph on Krejcar, Teige discounted this influence and highly praised Krejcar's design because he saw in it a model of collective housing and a harbinger of the future social system: "Well, transform this hotel for convalescents into a dwelling of workers; make the hotel rooms apartments for singles, that is, a dwelling without a household or household economy, a dwelling without kitchen; turn the wing with a restaurant and conference rooms into a tenants' club with a cafeteria, a din-

Photographer unknown

Machnáč Sanatorium, Trenčianske Teplice, 1930s

Architect Jaromír Krejcar, 1929–32

Private collection

Photographer unknown
Machnáč Sanatorium, Trenčianske Teplice, c. 1933
Architect Jaromír Krejcar, 1929–32
In: Karel Teige: *Práce Jaromíra Krejcara.*
Praha: 1933, p. 95, 96

ing room and a maternity ward, and you have a quite precise image of the collective dwelling, with centralized economy, cultural and social institutions [...]"[123]

Understandably, most people did not view the sanatorium in this way. As postcards sent by their guests and clients indicate, sanatoriums and spas were seen as places of recovery, cure, regeneration, rejuvenation, or even social diversion. Their distance from the urban environment and the context of everyday life reflected the belief in the curative power of nature, fresh air, sunlight and water. To bring people closer to nature, sanatoriums were most frequently located in the vicinity of springs (Karlovy Lázně, Mariánské Lázně, Luhačovice, Trenčianske Teplice, Sliač). Mountains were another favorite location of sanatoriums; characteristically, the subject of the largest international competition in architectural design in interwar Czechoslovakia was the sanatorium in Vyšné Hágy in the Tatra Mountains (1932). The use of the terrace and the balcony was the most visible expression of the effort to access fresh air and sunlight. Leading photographers such as Jaromír Funke and Jan Lukas highlighted these themes in their pictures of sanatoriums. Both Funke's pictures of the sanatorium building in Poděbrady (c. 1940) and Lukas's pictures of the Morava Sanatorium in Tatranská Lomnica designed by Bohuslav Fuchs in 1931 show a young woman sunbathing on the balcony or the terrace. The photographers promoted the healthy effect of the sun and air identified with the sanatorium by using the motif of the female body and making architectural photography indistinguishable from advertising.

Studio de Sandalo
Morava Sanatorium, Tatranská Lomnica,
c. 1932
Architect Bohuslav Fuchs, 1931
Brno City Museum, Architecture Collection

Jan Lukas ▸
Untitled (Morava Sanatorium, Tatranská Lomnica), 1931
Architect Bohuslav Fuchs, 1931
Brno City Museum, Architecture Collection

Jaromír Funke
May Sanatorium, Poděbrady, c. 1940
Architect Josef Havlíček, 1936–40
Private collection

Jan Lukas
*Untitled (Morava Sanatorium, Tatranská
Lomnica),* 1931
Architect Bohuslav Fuchs, 1931
Brno City Museum, Architecture Collection

swimming
pools

A heightened awareness of physical education, sport, and
recreation appears to be a natural reaction and a weapon
against an unhealthy way of life and the woeful environment
in which we live.

Václav Kolátor, "Buildings for Physical Education, and
Sport Recreation [Budovy pro tělovýchovnou a sportovní
rekreaci]," 1940

swimming
p o o l s

In his celebrated novella *Quirky Summer* [Rozmarné léto], (1926) Vladislav Vančura, a founding member of Devětsil, located its narrative at a public baths of a kind that one could find in almost every small town—a modest facility that consisted of light buildings made out of wood. The rise and spread of public baths and outdoor pools started in the 19th century with the growth of the middle class, a link which is manifested in *Quirky Summer's* main characters, a major, a priest, and the baths' owner. The spread of public baths and pools took off with the popularization of hygiene and physical exercise in the open air promoted by the reform movement, and echoed in Vančura's novella where the baths owner explains the benefits of his establishment: "Since the skin [...] is made to breathe and demands it very much. Sanitary opinions were instilled into my mind, I have accepted them and followed them with great benefits for my body."[124]

Baths and swimming pools represented one of several genres of vernacular architecture which the Devětsil architects found inspiring in the early 1920s. Vít Obrtel's *Project for a Rowing Club* (1922) is a typical example of early Devětsil works in which vernacular themes are intertwined with elements of nautical architecture popular among Czech architects thanks to Le Corbusier's example.[125] A functionalist version of this fusion of vernacular architecture and nautical elements appeared in the municipal baths in Brno-Zábrdovice (1929–31) designed by Bohuslav Fuchs. This structure, which was open to the public in both the summer and the winter, included swimming pools and sporting grounds complemented with various services. Its functional character was praised by critics who emphasized the primacy of function in architecture, especially by Karel Teige who named it among "the most consequential modern buildings" of contemporary Central and Western European architecture.[126] Studio de Sandalo made an extensive series of photographs of the baths' exterior and interior which were instrumental in publicizing the building in architectural journals and pictorial magazines. Sandalo also took pictures of Fuchs's municipal baths at Brno-Staré Brno (1927); its photographs represent a detailed documentation which covered both architectural and technical details, including showers, toilet bowls and sinks, pumps, pipes, and heating ducts. Fuchs used some of these pictures in his architectural collages which he exhibited at the important *Film und Foto* exhibition in Stuttgart in 1929. Two other Czech architects, Josef Hausenblas and Zdeněk Rossmann, also participated in the exhibition.[127]

The theme of swimming pools and baths became popular in avant-garde photography as well as in illustrated magazines at around the same time. For instance, the cover of the illustrated weekly *Domov a svět* [Home and Abroad] from August 3, 1929 featured a photograph by Jaromír Funke with the captions "Long Live the Swimming Pools!" and "This is Heaven!" which shows an older man in a swimming suit looking very much like a character from Vančura's *Quirky Summer*, complemented with a picture of a young woman in a swimming suit on the back cover. Several years later, when Funke was teaching photography at the State School of Graphic Arts, his students such as Staša Jílovská also took an interest in swimmers and sunbathers at Prague's baths and pools. Ada Novák, a member of the group Linie, took close-ups of baths and a reinforced concrete pool. Deemed especially photogenic, the theme of diving

Studio de Sandalo
Municipal Baths, Brno-Zábrdovice, c. 1931
Architect Bohuslav Fuchs, 1929–31
Brno City Museum, Architecture Collection

attracted numerous photographers, including Josef Voříšek and Karel Hájek, and was publicized by illustrated magazines.[128]

Prague's largest swimming pool of the time was designed by Václav Kolátor and built at a scenic site under the Barrandov Terraces in 1929–30.[129] It served as a swimming stadium for national swimming competitions and boasted the highest diving tower in Prague. Like the terraces above, the pool appeared in the photographs by Josef Sudek and Eugen Wiškovský taken from a bird's-eye view which corresponded with the popular theme of diving. The striking construction of the diving tower with a spiral staircase became an icon of water sports and an architectural emblem of the whole genre of building types designated as sporting facilities. It appeared on the cover of Kolátor's book *Baths* [Lázně] (1935) as well as in a collage by Karel Teige in 1941.[130] The Barrandov swimming pool was also the subject of the collage *Prague's Baths* (1932) by the architect Karel Lodr which represents a composite representation comprised of a Prague map and various views of the pool, including its aerial view and a close-up of a girl in a swimming suit.

Václav Kolátor, the architect of the Barrandov pool, also designed the swimming pools in Piešťany (together with F. Wimmer and A. Szönyi) (1934) and in Česká Třebová (1938). Among other architects who contributed to this field were Pavel Janák (Municipal Baths in Náchod, 1932), Oldřich Liska (Municipal Baths in Hradec Králové, 1933), and especially Bohuslav Fuchs who, besides the Municipal Baths in Brno-Zábrdovice designed the thermal swimming pool called 'Green Frog' [Zelená žába] in Trenčianske Teplice (1937). With its organic forms and elongated plan, Fuchs's building is integrated into its natural setting in the way that suggests

Studio de Sandalo

Municipal Baths, Brno-Zábrdovice, c. 1931
Architect Bohuslav Fuchs, 1929–31
Brno City Museum, Architecture Collection

Studio de Sandalo ▸

Municipal Baths (Water Massage), Brno-Zábrdovice, c. 1931
Architect Bohuslav Fuchs, 1929–31
Brno City Museum, Architecture Collection

Bohuslav Fuchs

Municipal Baths, Brno-Staré Brno, 1927–29

Collage

Brno City Museum, Architecture Collection

Studio de Sandalo

Municipal Baths (Sauna), Brno-Zábrdovice, c. 1931

Architect Bohuslav Fuchs, 1929–31

Brno City Museum, Architecture Collection

Photographer unknown

Swimming Pool, Moravské Budějovice,
1930s
Architect unknown, 1935
Private collection

Photographer unknown

Swimming Pool, Špindlerův Mlýn, 1930s
Architect unknown, 1933
Private collection

Ada Novák
Untitled (Swimming Pool), 1932
Private collection

a respect for the physical character of the site as well as a sense of the unique nature of the place. Unlike swimming pools, which could be built almost at any site, thermal pools and springs were places with long traditions and thus endowed with a symbolic status reflecting man's relation to nature, and how this relation had been changing. In his article on water sports in 1929, the painter and writer Emil Artur Pittermann-Longen described an attitude to nature which was typical for the time: "Modern life preaches a return to nature, but it does so in a practical sense to utilize all healthful possibilities in nature for regenerating one's forces, not in a romantic sense to reject civilization and culture and become a natural primitive again."[131] This instrumental notion of nature could result in the lack of understanding of (or even in a disregard of) the specific character of a particular location.

On the other hand, the outdoor location of swimming pools also inspired architects to take advantage of its unique characteristics and made them central to their design. In these cases, architectural design bordered on landscaping by working with elements that constituted the nature of the place, including its history and memory, in spite of the fact that the concept of *genius loci* was anathema to the new architecture. Photographs were instrumental in strengthening the memory of places and in distributing their images through space and time. Pictures of virtually every swimming pool were taken and circulated in the form of postcards, reflecting individual memories related to a specific place. Postcards of swimming pools which were produced in large number thus represent not only valuable documents of particular places but also a piece of architectural, cultural, and social history.

Eugen Wiškovský
The Barrandov Terraces, Prague (Swimming Pool, Prague-Barrandov), 1930s
Private collection

Josef Sudek ▸
Untitled (Swimming Pool, Prague-Barrandov), 1930s
Václav Kolátor, 1929–30
Private collection

c a f é s

[...] the modern public which, thanks to the promotion of Neue Sachlichkeit and functional interior design, prefers a café environment designed in a modern and functional rather than historical style.

Jan E. Koula, "New Cafés of Prague [Nové pražské kavárny]," 1933–34

c a f é s

In the chapter "The Cafés of Devětsil" of Karel Honzík's memoirs, he recalled: "These quiet places witnessed loud debates called into order by irritated newspaper readers or waiters. Here used to be the famed Národní kavárna [National Café], the main harbor of the Devětsil group in the years 1923 and 1924. Here the opinions of the combative purism and poetism formed at several marble tables in the café which, after a while, we called NARKAV for short."[132] Honzík's recollection may suggest that vintage photographs of café interiors, which are usually devoid of people, miss something crucial. In the photographs, the café interiors look like quiet places, although, as Honzík pointed out, their very essence was social intercourse.

Honzík noted that "a geography, not to mention a sociology, of Prague's cafés in the period between the two wars has not been written yet," although his reflections on the subject in the quoted chapter can be seen as a preliminary sketch of such "café geography" (if not sociology) that contains insights into various social functions of the café: "One would have to explain to today's reader of those sciences that cafés were not only luxurious facilities for loafers, but that they were also study rooms (when there was no heat at home or in one's sublet), as well as places for reading newspapers and books, and they were also clubs, conference rooms, and dating places. These refuges had a specific character depending on which of their purposes predominated and on the nature of their visitors."[133]

As Honzík reiterated, the café was a place of cultural interaction where avant-garde ideas were articulated, exchanged, and debated. This point has been made by a number of cultural historians who recognized in the café a symbolic locale linked to influential social, political, and cultural developments. It was a special place which enabled people to exchange their opinions in a manner that made it what one scholar aptly called "a stock exchange of opinions."[134] Honzík himself put forward a similar comparison in his description of the Národní kavárna: "In a small café space (6 x 20 m) there emerged a ground-plan of world-outlooks which then competed for the soul of the Czechoslovak citizen [...] You saw almost all of those searching for something in art or in science pass through this café, and many times even guests from far away, seekers from all of Europe passed through here."[135]

Honzík also noted how closely the café was linked with the notion of the "lively city," with the pulse of metropolitan life which was so dear to the Devětsil artists in general and to its architects in particular: "In the 1930s, almost the whole of Wenceslas Square up to the second floor (or even higher) was lined with cafés; their spaces penetrated at the rear into courtyards, into the city block and adjacent main avenues, so that if one were to demolish the wall that separated them, it would be possible to walk through almost the entire center of Prague as if it were a single café. Although this is an exaggeration, it is not far from the truth."[136]

Typically, cafés occupied fronts of various, most frequently late 19th-century and early 20th-century buildings. New cafés often originated as conversions or adaptations of the ground floor or the first floor of already existing buildings and followed the example of cafés built before World War I such as Café Arco (1907) by Jan Kotěra. There were also new buildings such as hotels, theaters, apartment and office buildings equipped with cafés, but there were only a few new cafés designed as single-purpose buildings. One of these exceptions was Café

Photographer unknown
Café Savoy, Brno City Center, c. 1929
Jindřich Kumpošt, 1928–29
Private collection

Era in Brno (1927–29) designed by Josef Kranz, a signature work of the young architect which was included in the exhibition of the International Style organized by the Museum of Modern Art in New York in 1932.[137] The asymmetrical composition of Café Era's façade evokes an abstract geometric painting as well as a book cover design in the style of new typography, as it highlights a typographical element in its signage (which was elaborated even more in the original project). The building also included interesting details such as several different types of windows and a curvilinear staircase that gave the café's interior a lyrical accent. These elements are documented by photographs which were carefully cropped and retouched by the architect, and preserved in his estate.

Brno boasted a number of other modern cafés designed by its leading architects, including Bohuslav Fuchs, Arnošt Wiesner, Jindřich Kumpošt, and Emil Králík. Most of them were located in the city center, such as the Café of Josef Zeman (1925) designed by Fuchs, one of the earliest examples of the purist style in Brno. Café Avion was a popular hang-out of avant-garde artists, including members of the Brno branch of Devětsil; it occupied the first and second floors of the Avion Hotel (1926–27) designed by Fuchs, which became an icon of the new Brno architecture. On the other hand, Café Esplanade (1925-26) by Arnošt Wiesner and Café Savoy (1928–29) by Jindřich Kumpošt were conversions of the ground and first floors of 19th-century buildings. Wiesner also designed the Morava building (1926–29, 1933, 1936) with a program similar to Krejcar's Olympic building in Prague, which included stores on the ground floor, a cinema in the underground, a café on the first floor, and administrative offices on the

upper floors. Its site, however, was more challenging and inspired the architect to create a complex and ingenious design that combined different plans for the ground and first floors on one hand and the upper floors on the other as the building's volume above the first floor curved inside to provide more light and air.[138]

The most interesting pictures of café interiors in Prague were taken by Josef Sudek. One of them was Café Juliš located at the eponymous hotel (1928–32) in Prague's Wenceslas Square, designed by Pavel Janák. Occupying the hotel's first floor and mezzanine, the café's interior was dominated by a curvilinear balcony lined with a tubular balustrade. In his pictures, Sudek focused on the changing relationship between the balcony's curve and the interior's rectangular grid, expressing a feeling of motion in space.

Sudek also took a series of pictures of the Barrandov Terraces Café and Restaurant (1927–29) in Prague-Barrandov which used an indoor and outdoor setting with a scenic view, combining modern architecture with landscaping. Located on a rock over the Vltava River in a suburb of Prague, this café and restaurant were designed by Max Urban for the real estate developer Václav Havel. Urban also designed the master plan of the district's development for

Josef Sudek
The Barrandov Terraces, Prague-Barrandov, c. 1930
Architect Max Urban, 1927–29
Museum of Decorative Arts, Prague

Josef Sudek ▸
The Barrandov Terraces, Prague-Barrandov, c. 1930
Architect Max Urban, 1927–29
Museum of Decorative Arts, Prague

Jan Lauschmann

At Barrandov, 1932

Architect Max Urban, 1927–29

Moravian Gallery, Brno

Josef Sudek

The Barrandov Terraces, Prague-Barrandov,

c. 1930

Architect Max Urban, 1927–29

Private collection

Havel which included a villa quarter and the A-B Film Studios in Prague-Barrandov. Sudek's photographs were commissioned by Havel for promotional purposes, including a flyer/brochure which was designed by Ladislav Kolda, an independent film producer and a few years later head of Baťa film production.[139]

The flyer juxtaposed Sudek's pictures with an advertising text in four languages,[140] describing the Terraces as "the Semiramis Gardens of Prague" and "one of the showplaces of the whole of Central Europe": "Here you will find a restaurant with exquisite French dishes brought to you by French chefs, as well as a café and additional restaurant with popular prices. The building is surrounded by an open-air amphitheater accommodating 3,500 guests. It is an enchanting place that overlooks the Vltava River and the adjacent foothills. Below the steep rock on which Barrandov is erected, is the large swimming pool of the CPK water sport society. Away from the hectic city, the terraces of Barrandov are a unique refuge and a source of enjoyment in its modest modern forms."

The flyer's cover featured a bird's-eye view of the Terraces filled with chairs and tables seen from the café/restaurant tower, a motif that became very popular with Czech photographers. In the 1930s, the Terraces appeared in pictures taken, among others, by Jan Lauschmann, Arnošt Pikart, Drahomír Růžička, Josef Ehm, and Julius Tutsch, becoming one of the signature motifs of new photography in Czechoslovakia.[141]

family
houses

Studio de Sandalo
Slavík House, Brno-Žabovřesky, c. 1931
Architect Josef Kranz, 1930–31
Private collection

The problem of housing is one of the most burning contemporary issues; it is very valuable for architectural and social development that modern architects devote so much effort to overcoming all the prejudices accumulated over the ages, and contributing to the evolution of modern man [...]

Oldřich Starý, "The 'New House' Colony [Kolonie 'Nový dům']," 1929

f a m i l y
h o u s e s

The first important projects and realizations of the Devětsil architects Jaromír Krejcar, Evžen Linhart, Karel Honzík, and Josef Havlíček were family houses such as the Vančura House (1924–26) by Krejcar, the Jíša House in Prague-Smíchov (1928–29) by Honzík and Havlíček, and Linhart's own house (1927–29) or his remodeling of the villa in Praha-Hostivař (1925–27). This was also the case of Jiří Kroha, who designed two villas in Kosmonosy (1923–24) and his own house in Brno (1928–29). Typically, architects first designed modern houses for their friends or for themselves. Architects' own houses, such as Kroha's house and Bohumil Fuchs's house in Brno (1927–28) and Linhart's house and Josef Karel Říha's house in Prague (1929–30) served as a showcase of the new architecture and were publicized in both architectural and popular magazines.

The privileged position of the family house in the development of the new architecture stemmed from different reasons. It reflected the symbolic value of this building type, which in the eyes of the general public represented the primary function of architecture—dwelling. Another reason was the fact that it was easier to find clients for innovative family house designs, most frequently among friends and supporters. As the architect Oldřich Starý pointed out, the less restrictive regulations involved in building family houses also played a role: "To realize even the most extreme conceptions, it was relatively easy to test different building methods and possibilities on which all innovative work of architects drew, and did not imply major financial expenditure or zoning consequences."[142]

But the privileged position of the family house associated with the original function of architecture was also the very same reason why even small changes in the look and concep-tion of the family house were resisted by the general public. As a consequence, proponents of the new architecture realized that public opinion had to be won over for their cause—that public relations constituted a key element of their project. It was this need to influence and educate public opinion that inspired the rise of modern housing exhibitions in the form of model settlements. Oldřich Starý, one of the organizers of the *Exhibition of New Housing; Baba Set-tlement, Prague* (1932) stated: "It is necessary to accustom and persuade the general public about a number of things whose reception has not yet been achieved in our country, be it a new building method, a new construction element, a ground-plan detail or a view of the function of individual elements of the dwelling."[143]

The first exhibition of modern housing, which took place in Brno under the title the *New House Exhibition*, was organized under the auspices of the Czechoslovak Werkbund [Svaz československého díla] as part of the *Exhibition of Contemporary Culture in Czechoslovakia* in 1928. It opened only a year after the Weissenhofsiedlung in Stuttgart—a pilgrimage site for pro-ponents of modern architecture and a source of inspiration for later similar projects. The Brno exhibition consisted of sixteen houses of nine different family-house types designed primarily by architects based in Brno, including Bohuslav Fuchs, Jaroslav Grunt, Jiří Kroha, Jan Víšek, and Arnošt Wiesner. Although this local focus was the reason why the exhibition did not receive attention in foreign professional publications, the project was a major achievement for the city, which until 1918 had been a mere provincial town of the Hapsburg monarchy. But a successful

Photographer unknown
Three-Unit Family House at the New House Colony, Brno-Žabovřesky, 1928
Architect Jaroslav Grunt, 1927–28
Private collection

Štenc Graphic Enterprise
Baba Settlement, Prague-Dejvice, 1932
Štenc Archive, Prague

business venture it was not: not a single house was sold during the exhibition, and the developer who financed the project was forced into bankruptcy.[144]

In November 1928, shortly after the Brno exhibition closed, the Czechoslovak Werkbund initiated the Baba Settlement project. The goal of the exhibition, which opened in September 1932, was to demonstrate that modern housing was, in the organizers' words, "functional, healthy, pretty, and reasonable."[145]

The advertising leaflet from 1931 boasted that the houses were "designed to the last element of the roof and garden, simply and democratically, with regards to all developments which have emerged in housing design, especially abroad, and to which our public is also entitled."[146] The organizers also saw the exhibition as a link between other similar projects in Central Europe, notably in Vienna and Berlin. To avoid the financial loss incurred by the previous exhibition, clients were selected from the Werkbund members and their friends who erected family houses mostly for themselves at their own cost.

The exhibition's mission was to promote new architectural ideas in the field of housing and to provide viable examples which the public could follow, as the following statement by organizers of the Baba Settlement indicates: "The settlement should be an example and aid for other similar action projects and it should be regarded as a collection of types, well thought-out and elaborated in its building program: ground-plan, from the point of construction; hygiene, with regards to interior furnishing; garden design; and also to the entire plastic solution, which is evaluated according to particularly strict criteria."[147]

Štenc Graphic Enterprise

Jíša House, Prague-Smíchov, 1929

Architects Josef Havlíček and Karel Honzík,

1928–29

Štenc Archive, Prague

Jaroslav Möller
Říha House, Prague-Smíchov, c. 1930
Architect Josef Karel Říha, 1929–30
Private collection

193

Štenc Graphic Enterprise
Fuchs House, Brno-Žabovřesky, 1928
Architect Bohuslav Fuchs, 1927–28
Štenc Archive, Prague

Štenc Graphic Enterprise
Fuchs House, Brno-Žabovřesky, 1928
Architect Bohuslav Fuchs, 1927–28
Štenc Archive, Prague

However, when the exhibition of the Baba Settlement started in September 1932, the economic and cultural situation changed considerably. The worldwide Depression caused a rise in unemployment and homelessness, and radicalized the political views of avant-garde artists. The Devětsil group ceased to exist and most its members joined the Left Front, an organization that identified with the political agenda of the Communist Party, organizing its activity in several sections.[148] In 1931 the Architectural Section of the Left Front organized the *Exhibition of Proletarian Housing*.[149] Even architects who were not members of left-wing organizations felt that they should participate in what they saw as the social priority of the time—in providing a healthy dwelling for all members of society, including those with a low income.

Karel Teige was a leading voice of this social direction in Czech architecture. Like Hannes Meyer and some other architects who identified with the radical political programs, he saw a solution in a new society based on social planning, in promoting new social forms such as collective living and housing, while criticizing capitalist society for being dominated by market forces. For this reason, he rejected the family house as an obsolete building type and criticized settlement exhibition projects such as the Baba Settlement: "[...] although one can expect that Baba will be an achievement of considerable architectural and technological significance, one cannot fail to see that the social problem of dwelling is posed here incorrectly and in an

Štenc Graphic Enterprise
Villa Tugendhat, Brno-Černá Pole, 1931
Architect Ludwig Mies van der Rohe,
1928–30
Štenc Archive, Prague

Štenc Graphic Enterprise

Villa Tugendhat, Brno-Černá Pole, 1931
Architect Ludwig Mies van der Rohe,
1928–30
Štenc Archive, Prague

Štenc Graphic Enterprise

Villa Tugendhat, Brno-Černá Pole, 1931
Architect Ludwig Mies van der Rohe,
1928–30
Brno City Museum, Architecture Collection

outdated way, and that building villas and family houses (even minimal houses) cannot solve the lack of housing."[150]

The organizers of the Baba Settlement Exhibition responded to this criticism by joining Teige in his expression of social concerns while arguing for a piecemeal approach. On one hand, they argued that the new architecture should "improve living conditions of all working people" and "not to engage oneself in an exclusive task, but in the elemental need of the masses." But, on the other hand, they suggested that the "calls for recreating cities, their residential quarters, for the most economical dwelling, for the solution of collective housing" associated with the notion that "we should not engage in anything else" should not overshadow the fact that "to achieve these major goals means enormous expenditures, zoning and real-estate transformations, legislative intervention, and the cooperation of the political representation and even the general public."[151]

Zdenka Pícková

*Modern Architecture (Auerbach House,
Praha-Barrandov),* c. 1935
Architects Herman Abeles and Leo Mayer,
1933–34
Private collection

František Illek ▷

Villa Hain, Prague-Vysočany, 1930s
Architect Ladislav Žák, 1932–33
Private collection

František Illek

Villa Hain, Prague-Vysočany, 1930s

Architect Ladislav Žák, 1932–33

Private collection

František Illek

Villa Hain, Prague-Vysočany, 1930s

Architect Ladislav Žák, 1932–33

Private collection

Jiří Kroha

Sociological Fragment of Housing, 1932–33
Collage
Brno City Museum, Architecture Collection

Karel Lodr ▶

Project for Temporary Housing, 1935
Collage
Private collection

This twofold response resulted in a certain disconnection between architectural theory and practice that characterized the work of many Czech avant-garde architects. Even proponents of the most radical social and political agendas such as the group PAS (Karel Janů, Jiří Štursa, and Jiří Voženílek) continued designing family villas for well-to-do members of the middle class. This contradiction, or more precisely the bad conscience that resulted from it, might explain why one of the most significant international examples of new architecture, the Villa Tugendhat in Brno (1928–30) designed by the German architect Ludwig Mies van der Rohe, was almost completely ignored by Czech architectural publications of the period. Without doubt, the project for the Tugendhat house represented an "exceptional task" that flew in the face of socially-minded Czech architects.

Byt a umění [Dwelling and Art] was the only Czech architectural journal which devoted substantial space to the Villa Tugendhat in one of its issues in 1932.[152] The magazine's cover featured a photograph of the living room that highlighted cruciform chrome plated columns as a signature element of the building. This and other pictures of the Villa Tugendhat reproduced in *Byt a umění* and elsewhere stressed the precision of details and the preciousness of materials such as the onyx wall dividing the living room and the screen of Macassar ebony partially separating the dining area. For the most part, they were authored by Studio de Sandalo, who took many architectural pictures in Brno and Prague. Another series of pictures of the Villa Tugendhat was taken by the Štenc Graphic Enterprise.

The contrast between the Czech architects' social views on housing and their own architectural practice is exemplified by the work of Ladislav Žák. As an architect and furniture designer,

Hugo Táborský
Untitled (Family House, Brno-Stránice), c. 1936
Architect František Kalivoda, 1935–36
Private collection

Hugo Táborský

Untitled (Family House, Brno-Stránice), c. 1936
Negative reticulation
Architect František Kalivoda, 1935–36
Private collection

Žák designed a number of family houses and villas that epitomized a sophisticated functional style characterized by Czech critics as 'emotional functionalism' as it reflected more the complexity of an individual's needs than the needs of a collective. For example, the previously mentioned Villa Hain in Prague had amenities such as a glazed conservatory, a cantilevered sun terrace and a built-in sand pit, as well as a flag pole placed on a cantilevered crow's nest accessible from the terrace by a companion stairway. This was a far cry from scientific and social reductionism preached not only by Teige but often also by Czech architects themselves.[153]

Besides Teige's publication *Nejmenší byt* [Minimum Dwelling] (1932), the set of didactic tables titled *Sociologický fragment bydlení* [Sociological Fragment of Housing] (1932–33) created by Jiří Kroha with his students represents perhaps the most striking example of the tendency to merge architecture with social theory by combining didactic text with photomontages, diagrams and statistics.[154] Left Front architects employed a similar method in the *Exhibition of Proletarian Housing* (1931) which heralded the popularity of social themes with Czech photographers. Many avant-garde architects and photographers shared the same social and political concerns in the 1930s, following ideas advanced by the critic and theoretician Karel Teige. Lubomír Linhart, a film and photography critic, played a similar role by criticizing avant-garde photography as bourgeois formalism and promoted the concepts of social and socialist photography whose mission was to advance political goals of the Communist Party.[155] In 1933 and 1934 Linhart organized for the Left Front two exhibitions of social photography in which homelessness and unemployment were the most frequent subjects, echoing the social themes of the earlier *Exhibition of Proletarian Housing*.[156]

Hugo Táborský

Untitled (Family House, Brno-Stránice), c. 1936
Negative reticulation
Architect František Kalivoda, 1935–36
Private collection

Žák designed a number of family houses and villas that epitomized a sophisticated functional style characterized by Czech critics as 'emotional functionalism' as it reflected more the complexity of an individual's needs than the needs of a collective. For example, the previously mentioned Villa Hain in Prague had amenities such as a glazed conservatory, a cantilevered sun terrace and a built-in sand pit, as well as a flag pole placed on a cantilevered crow's nest accessible from the terrace by a companion stairway. This was a far cry from scientific and social reductionism preached not only by Teige but often also by Czech architects themselves.[153]

Besides Teige's publication *Nejmenší byt* [Minimum Dwelling] (1932), the set of didactic tables titled *Sociologický fragment bydlení* [Sociological Fragment of Housing) (1932–33) created by Jiří Kroha with his students represents perhaps the most striking example of the tendency to merge architecture with social theory by combining didactic text with photomontages, diagrams and statistics.[154] Left Front architects employed a similar method in the *Exhibition of Proletarian Housing* (1931) which heralded the popularity of social themes with Czech photographers. Many avant-garde architects and photographers shared the same social and political concerns in the 1930s, following ideas advanced by the critic and theoretician Karel Teige. Lubomír Linhart, a film and photography critic, played a similar role by criticizing avant-garde photography as bourgeois formalism and promoted the concepts of social and socialist photography whose mission was to advance political goals of the Communist Party.[155] In 1933 and 1934 Linhart organized for the Left Front two exhibitions of social photography in which homelessness and unemployment were the most frequent subjects, echoing the social themes of the earlier *Exhibition of Proletarian Housing.*[156]

c h u r c h e s

The Czech-Moravian Evangelical Church in Brno by Jan Víšek
from 1928 was the first and, for a long time, the only modern
church building, simple and harmonious.

Jan E. Koula, *New Czech Architecture and Its Develop-*
***ment in the Twentieth Century* [Nová česká architektura**
a její vývoj ve XX. století], 1940

c h u r c h e s

In 1941 Břetislav Štorm, a writer and specialist in design of liturgical objects, published a treatise entitled *Architektura a pokrok* [Architecture and Progress] which examined the church as a building type from a traditionalist position, advancing a critique of modern architecture. Štorm criticized the modern "disrespect for invariant values" which, according to him, had "brought about a splitting into a great number of movements and currents," "uprooted the natural relationships between the spirit and matter," and "installed the rule of dumb, heedless technology." The loss of man's "rule over matter" supposedly "caused a chaos in the building industry" and as a result, "nothing has had its proper name": "The house has become a machine for dwelling [...] the brick has become a cinder block, light has become the radiance of the wall, and the church has become an architectural issue."[157]

Unlike the building types that originated in the 19th century and symbolized innovation and technological progress, the church was a symbol of continuity, implying a reverence for the past. This characteristic presented a challenge to proponents of new architecture who were firm believers in innovation and progress. It also fostered different and often conflicting architectural interpretations of the church and conditioned specific pitfalls of this building type. The tendency to overemphasize traditional concerns ran risks of transforming the church into a museum, while stressing new construction methods and building materials which did not take into account the church's unique function made the church look like a factory or a meeting hall.[158]

For all these risks, the modern movement did not shy away from the field of sacral architecture. On the contrary, there were numerous new church buildings not only in big cities but also in small towns of interwar Czechoslovakia which were informed by the vocabulary of the new architecture. These realizations were commissioned by various denominations, but the most frequent client among them was the Czechoslovak Evangelical Church of the Protestant denomination which was influenced by writings of the first Czechoslovak president Tomáš Garrigue Masaryk. Significantly, one of the early important examples of modern sacral architecture was the Jan Hus Congregation of the Czechoslovak Evangelical Church in Brno (1926–28) designed by Jan Víšek, a proponent of purism in architecture. Its building consists of carefully proportioned and differentiated volumes devoid of any decorative elements. By highlighting large pure surfaces of the interior and exterior, photographs of the building preserved in the Štenc Archives underlined the purist concept of the building which corresponded with the Protestant iconoclastic tradition.

In the same years, Josef Gočár designed the Ambrose Congregation of the Czechoslovak Evangelical Church in Hradec Králové which was built on a V-shaped site. This form inspired the church's innovative plan whose elements also appeared in Gočár's design of the reinforced concrete St. Wenceslas Roman Catholic church in Prague-Vršovice (1927–30). Shortly after the building was finished, Josef Sudek took some of the most interesting architectural photographs of the period, among the most successful representations of a modern church interior exploring the role played by light in co-creating sacral space. Sudek's previous involvement in the movement of pictorialist photography, whose central

Photographer unknown
*Ambrosius Congregation of the
Czechoslovak Evangelical Church,
Hradec Králové,* c. 1929
Architect Josef Gočár, 1926–29
Private collection

Photographer unknown
*St. Wenceslas Church,
Prague-Vršovice,* 1930s
Architect Josef Gočár, 1927–30
Private collection

Photographer unknown ▸
*St. Wenceslas Church,
Prague-Vršovice,* 1930s
Architect Josef Gočár, 1927–30
Private collection

Arno Pařík (?)
St. Wenceslas Church, Prague-Vršovice, c. 1930
Architect Josef Gočár, 1927–30
Private collection

Josef Sudek
St. Wenceslas Church, Prague-Vršovice, c. 1930
Architect Josef Gočár, 1927–30
Private collection

Josef Sudek
St. Wenceslas Church, Prague-Vršovice, c. 1930
Architect Josef Gočár, 1927–30
Private collection

Josef Sudek
St. Wenceslas Church, Prague-Vršovice, c. 1930
Architect Josef Gočár, 1927–30
Private collection

Photographer unknown
*Hus Congregation of the Czechoslovak
Evangelical Church, Dobruška*, 1930s
Architects Otto Kubeček and Václav Steklík,
1935–36
Private collection

Photographer unknown
*Hus Congregation of the Czechoslovak
Evangelical Church, Nové Město nad Metují*,
1930s
Architect Jindřich Freiwald, 1932–33
Private collection

Photographer unknown
*Hus Congregation of the Czechoslovak
Evangelical Church, Prague-Vinohrady*,
c. 1933
Architect Pavel Janák, 1931–33
National Technical Museum, Prague

theme was the play of light and shadows, served him well for this assignment. In his work, Gočár learned a lesson from other churches' use of light, notably from an example provided by the famous church at Le Raincy near Paris (1922–23) designed by Auguste Perret. One of the earliest reinforced concrete structures with stained glass windows, this building was enormously influential, but also criticized for its fenestration which runs around both the naves and the choir, failing to emphasize the liturgical function of the choir and the altar.[159] Gočár eliminated the nave windows and used a conically shaped plan to amplify the effect of perspective, guiding the eyes to the altar and the stained windows in the choir. He also took advantage of the rising terrain on which the church was erected by creating cascading grades in the ceiling which provided indirect top lighting. By giving prominence to natural lighting and the role of perspective, Sudek's pictures captured the essence of Gočár's ingenious design.

The Hus Congregation of the Czechoslovak Evangelical Church in Prague-Vinohrady (1931–33) designed by Pavel Janák represents another distinct example of sacral architecture. It consists of three units, a house of worship with a columbarium, an apartment building, and a tower with a spiral staircase culminating in the church emblem in the form of a chalice. The reinforced concrete tower structure demonstrates that sacral architecture could effectively utilize new building methods and the vocabulary of the new architecture. Much less successful in this respect is the exterior of the house of worship, which looks almost like an industrial building, a point made about modern sacral architecture by various critics, including Břetislav Štorm.[160]

Erected in the same neighborhood and finished in the same years, the Church of the Sacred Heart of Jesus (1928–32, designed 1922–28) by Josip Plečnik is a very different example of sacral architecture. Plečnik's design clearly communicates the building's function by using numerous references to the tradition of sacral architecture while its interpretation is not antiquarian or conservative. Its idiosyncratic style adopts elements of various historical periods, especially of classical antiquity, while thriving on the innovative and often unexpected use of materials as well as on the high quality of workmanship. Resembling an ancient ship, the church culminates in a massive bell tower of unusual design which houses a large glass clock and a ramp leading between its dials up to the top. For all its modern originality, the tower's monumental character, which is manifested in Josef Voříšek's photograph taken from an oblique angle, indicates that Plečnik's frame of reference was the mediterranean classical tradition, not the industrial revolution.[161]

Unlike the church, the crematorium represented a new building type that resulted from the modernization of the funeral rite. In this respect it is significant that the crematorium in Nymburk (1922–24) by Bedřich Feuerstein and Bohumil Sláma was widely publicized as one the first buildings identified with the aesthetic of purism and the modern movement in architecture. The rising popularity of cremation was inspired by the concept of hygiene which sanitized the traditional ritual. Arnošt Wiesner, who designed the crematorium in Brno-Bohunice (1925–30, 1932–33), the most accomplished work of this genre in interwar Czechoslovakia, defined precisely the peculiar character of the new building type: "Our age which seeks to get rid of religious ritual—in the effort of penetrating the depth of every feeling—has again come to cremation. [...] with its effort at abstraction, technical form, the technical apparatus used for cremation today interferes and does not allow that ideational release that the last moments of an individual's earthly existence should elicit in survivors. It is certain that today's cremating process precedes the creation of a new cult, and that this cult will emerge only when our time —technology and art—finds its expression matching the cult of previous times in its internal and external greatness."[162]

The precise understanding and definition of his task guided Wiesner in articulating an organization of space which followed strictly functional requirements of both the ritual and the cremation process. His goal was to create a type in which ground-plan and building represent a complete unity and which does not allow any variability of its main features. The central idea of the architect's concept was to eliminate any profane elements and to separate strictly the ritual and the actual cremating process, as well as their individual units. According to him, the space for the ritual "cannot be a hall or a church-like room in any way but only a place closed off from the outside,"[163] an internal top-lit court with no windows, lit from large glass plates in the ceiling—from the sky. As the crematorium's pictures demonstrate, the same idea was expressed in the structure's exterior by contrasting the dark horizontal base with the white vertical courtyard whose pillars point to the sky. The pyramidal ending of the pillars and their placement around the court refer to the Christian church and the Egyptian pyramid, two forms mentioned by Wiesner as examples of the highest form of the cult.[164] Wiesner's crematorium thus represents an ambitious attempt to develop a modern equivalent of traditional types by using new building methods and forms in the service of the immaterial and to ground the new building type of the crematorium in a function that seemed improbable in the framework of the new architecture—transcendence.

Josef Voříšek
Bell Tower, Church of the Sacred Heart of Jesus, Prague-Vinohrady, 1930s
Architect Josip Plečnik, 1928–32
(designed 1922–28)
Private collection

Štenc Graphic Enterprise

Crematorium, Brno-Bohunise, 1930s
Architect Arnošt Wiesner, 1925–30,
1932–33
Štenc Archive, Prague

Photographer unknown

Crematorium, Brno-Bohunice, 1930s
Architect Arnošt Wiesner, 1925–30,
1932–33
National Technical Museum, Prague

architectural
details

Josef Sudek

Untitled (View from the Barrandov Terraces,
Prague-Barrandov), c. 1930
Architect Max Urban, 1927–29
Private collection

In the case of the window, we encounter the following questions that are necessary to clarify and solve: lighting by daylight, access to sunshine, ventilation, heat and sound insulation, window shading, the window opening (cleaning and waterproofing), construction (materials, types, mounting, etc.), associated constructions, standards and norms, and its appropriate use as an element with aesthetic (or even "psychological") effects on the interior space and exterior surface of the building.

Vojtěch Krch, The Window: A Part of the Building and Dwelling Interior [Okno: součást budovy a obytné míst-nosti], 1935

architectural
details

The general public identified new architecture with several features that seemed to be most striking: the flat roof, the horizontal window, the skeleton of steel and glass, and the angular structure devoid of decorative forms. In popular view, these elements and details became icons of new architecture and a modern life style—significant forms that conveyed a message of modernity. Photography was instrumental in this transformation by facilitating and amplifying symbolic readings and making them accessible to the widest audience.

The famous dictum "Form follows function," coined by the American architect Louis Sullivan in the second half of the 19th century, emerged as the central slogan of the modern movement in architecture in the 1920s and 1930s. Together with other well-known statements, Adolf Loos's "Ornament is crime" and Ludwig Mies van der Rohe's "Less is more," it advanced the rejection of classical architectural elements and of the rhetorical notion of architecture. However, the concept of functionalism created a new narrative manifested in the production of new images, in the preference for certain materials, technologies, forms, and building types. New buildings, their individual forms and details conveyed a story of progress and a better world, evoking a grand narrative of modernity.

No other architectural form demonstrates this symbolic potential of detail more than the window thanks to its prominent position in the history of architecture as well as in the evolution of Western pictorial representation. Compared to the picture frame since the Renaissance, the window has been encoded in the construction of pictorial space (and, consequently, in photographic and cinematic apparatuses), as numerous treatises on linear perspective indicated. The window is not only one of many architectural details but a privileged form that foregrounds the visuality of architecture by relating it to the viewer's body. The window is an embodiment of sight as well as an early example of a framing device that enables the viewer to create a narrative out of individual fragments, providing a metaphor for the camera's capacity to isolate significant details.

Because of its privileged position, the window received great attention from both architects and photographers. The horizontal window was seen as one of the signature elements of new architecture and the subject of numerous articles and photographs.[165] For instance, Sudek and Funke, two leading Czech photographers, explored the window theme in their architectural photographs, including two main types: vertically- and horizontally-proportioned windows. Sudek's picture of a vertical window is taken from the Barrandov Terraces Restaurant (1927–29) designed by Max Urban (see other photographs of the building in the chapter on cafés), which was part of the Barrandov quarter on the outskirts of Prague developed by Václav Havel (the father of the future Czech President). The window shows one of the restaurant terraces as well as a scenic view of the Vltava valley for which the restaurant became a popular destination for Prague middle-class outings. The window's metal frame divides and organizes pictorial space, evoking the act of composing an image in the camera's viewer, a theme that Sudek explored later in his series *View from the Window of My Studio* (1940–54), for which he became well-known.

Jaromír Funke
From the series *New Architecture (Masaryk Student Dormitory, Brno-Veveří)*, 1930
Architect Bohuslav Fuchs, 1929–30
Brno City Museum, Architecture Collection

Jaromír Funke

From the series *New Architecture (Masaryk Student Dormitory, Brno-Veveří)*, 1930

Architect Bohuslav Fuchs, 1929–30

Brno City Museum, Architecture Collection

Jaromír Funke
From the series *New Architecture (Masaryk Student Dormitory, Brno-Veveří),* 1930
Architect Bohuslav Fuchs, 1929–30
Brno City Museum, Architecture Collection

Jaromír Funke

From the series *New Architecture (Masaryk Student Dormitory, Brno-Veveří)*, 1930
Architect Bohuslav Fuchs, 1929–30
Brno City Museum, Architecture Collection

Photographer unknown

Untitled (Prague Electricity Board, Prague-Holešovice), 1930s
Architects Adolf Benš and Josef Kříž, 1927–35
Private collection

Funke's pictures of the Masaryk student dormitory in Brno designed by Bohuslav Fuchs (1929–30) represents the photographer's most extensive series devoted to modern architecture. One of the photographs depicts a horizontal window folded in the middle and opened at its sides. The shifting window planes and the picture's diagonal composition turn the window into a movable optical instrument, creating a complex geometry of intersecting frames—an interplay of flatness and depth, transparency and opacity reminiscent of Funke's early abstract pictures of glass plates.

Funke used diagonal compositions in his other pictures of the building exterior and interior; the photograph of the façade is the most well-known of the series as it appeared on the cover of the monograph on the building.[166] In its geometric counterpoint of flat and spatial forms, the photograph is similar to the photographer's pictures of the ESSO power plant in Kolín, but its overall character is more abstract. Funke's photographs of Fragner's power plant and Fuchs's student dormitories were part of his *New Architecture* series. Several years later when he became professor at the State School by Graphic Arts in Prague, Funke introduced

Jaromír Funke
From the series *New Architecture (Country
Exhibition of Physical Education and Sport
of the Czechoslovak Republic, Pardubice),* 1931
Karel Řepa, 1930–31
Private collection

Jaromír Funke
From the series *New Architecture (Country
Exhibition of Physical Education and Sport
of the Czechoslovak Republic, Pardubice),* 1931
Karel Řepa, 1930–31
Private collection

Ada Novák
Untitled (New Architecture in České Budějovice), 1932
Private collection

Ada Novák
Untitled (New Architecture in České Budějovice), 1932
Private collection

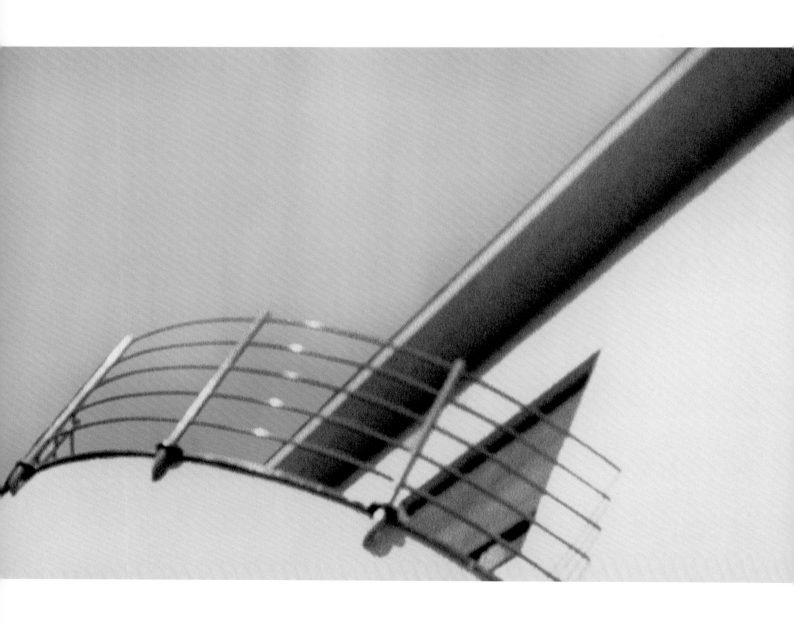

Ada Novák
Untitled (New Architecture in České Budějovice), 1932
Private collection

Ada Novák
Untitled (New Architecture in České Budějovice), 1932
Private collection

Karel Plicka

Zelená žába [Green Frog] Swimming Pool,
Trenčianske Teplice, c. 1936
Architect Bohuslav Fuchs 1935–36
Brno City Museum, Architecture Collection

Karel Plicka

Zelená žába [Green Frog] Swimming Pool,
Trenčianske Teplice, c. 1936
Architect Bohuslav Fuchs 1935–36
Brno City Museum, Architecture Collection

the photography of modern architecture into the school curriculum. Like Funke, his students also often used diagonal compositions in their photographs of modern architecture.

The work of Ada Novák, a member of the avant-garde group Linie in České Budějovice, represents another approach to modern architecture that consisted of multiple readings of architectural details. Some of his pictures are slightly out of focus, but they can hardly be characterized as pictorialist: their theme was not a "play of light and shadows," but a new interpretation of architectural details such as the cornice or the balcony, which were transformed into original studies of spatial forms.

The balcony was a popular subject in architectural photographs of the period. It frequently appeared in family houses, apartment buildings, and in sanatorium and spa buildings, manifesting the new architecture's quest for more light and air. The work of Bohuslav Fuchs represented one of the most significant examples of this pursuit. In his designs for spa and sanatorium buildings such as the Morava Sanatorium in Tatranská Lomnica (1931) or the

Josef Sudek

Untitled (Exhibition of the Construction Industry and Housing in Prague), 1932
Museum of Decorative Arts, Prague

František Illek ▸

Löbl Department Store Light Advertising, Prague-Old Town, c. 1934
Architect Zdeněk Pešánek, 1933–34
Private collection

Studio de Sandalo

Prague Electricity Board,
Prague-Holešovice, 1935
Architects Adolf Benš and Josef Kříž,
1927–35
Private collection

Josef Sudek
Staircase (ESSO Power Plant, Kolín), c. 1932
Architect Jaroslav Fragner, 1929–32
Private collection

swimming pool in Trenčianske Teplice (1935–36), Fuchs made the balcony and the terrace dominate the whole exterior of the building and open it to air and light as much as possible. The photographs of these buildings by Karel Plicka and Jan Lukas reflected the architect's effort to connect the outside and the inside by focusing on the balcony as the essence of the building.

The most visible architectural forms and details are located at street level. Entrances, passages, shop windows, kiosks, streetcar stops and stations, lamps, signs and signage in general are prominent elements of the urban environment. Since the avant-garde group Devětsil made the celebration of modern city life its central theme, it is not surprising that Czech architects paid great attention to such details. They seemed to have a special predilection for signs and signage in their designs, embracing vernacular styles of advertising lettering with unprecedented care, interest that would reappear in pop art in the late 1950s and 1960s. They were also very fond of electric and fluorescent lights, which in their view symbolized the vibrancy of city life.[167] The concept of the luminous city occupied leading

Jindřich (Heinrich) Koch
Tatra Car Showroom, Kolín, c. 1933
Architect Jaroslav Fragner, 1930–32
Private collection

Zdenka Pícková ▶
Modern Architecture (Auerbach House,
Prague-Barrandov), c. 1935
Architects Herman Abeles and Leo Mayer,
1933–34
Private collection

Josef Sudek

Staircase (Family House, Lipany), c. 1932

Architect Jan E. Koula, 1932

Private collection

Photographer unknown
Untitled, 1930s
Private collection

Studio de Sandalo
Apartment Building Nameplates, c. 1930
Private collection

Studio de Sandalo
Apartment Building, Bayerova Street,
Brno-Veveří, c. 1933
Architect Václav Dvořák (with V. and
A. Kubas), 1932–33
Brno City Museum, Architecture Collection

architects, including Josef Chochol who wrote an article on the subject titled "Prague Architecture of Light" in 1929.[168] In his important design for the Liberated Theater created two years earlier, Chochol rendered the building as it would appear at night, and on top of the building placed a spotlight, which was a popular motif among constructivist architects in Russia like for example the Vesnin brothers who incorporated it in their Pravda building in Leningrad.[169] Another key and widely publicized project of the period, Jaromír Krejcar's design for the Olympic building (1923–26) showed an electric light board that covered the entire side of the building.

Zdeněk Pešánek was the most important artist and architect who worked in the medium of artificial light. This pioneer of kinetic art made electric and fluorescent lights his primary medium while designing public kinetic sculptures as well as light advertising and designs for the urban environment. His design for light advertising signs for the Löbl Department Store in Prague (1933–34), which consisted of a vertical light tower on the building's corner and horizontal advertising signs in color, was one the most successful realizations in this field.[170] František Illek's photograph revealed the essence of Pešánek's design by presenting it as a monumental light sculpture.

The Czech artists' fondness for electric and fluorescent advertising signs is reflected in a number of pictures on the subject by photographers such as Funke, Josef Ehm, and Viktor Schück who used multiple exposures to convey the feeling of excitement and movement associated with the night life of the big city. Before this subject became popular in photography, it appeared in films and was discussed by architects and architectural critics.[171] The theme of big city life found its most eloquent medium in cinema. While there were a number of films on city life, the film titled *Prague Shining in Lights* (1928) by Svatopluk Innemann occupies a special position in this genre since its main character was artificial light.[172] The film, which chronicled city activities from dusk to dawn, was made in 1928 when the Prague Electricity Board organized *A Tribute to Light: To Prague* to celebrate the 10th anniversary of Czechoslovakia. On this occasion, the spectacular lighting of historical monuments and buildings transformed the city into one big stage, and this event was extensively documented by photographs and a special publication.[173] The element of spectacle produced by special lighting effects was also strongly present in major exhibitions and fairs such as the *Exhibition of Northern Bohemia* in Mladá Boleslav in 1927 and the *Exhibition of Contemporary Culture in Czechoslovakia* in Brno in 1928.

Photographers have a special understanding of how light, as well as a viewing angle, can dramatically change the character of the photographed object. If the object is a work of art, especially a complex spatial form such as a building or its detail, this understanding makes the photographer an interpreter who co-creates and re-creates the work of art by confirming or altering its established perception. The picture of a staircase by Josef Sudek (from the collection of the Museum of Fine Arts in Houston) represents a striking example of this transformative power of the photographer's vision: the staircase morphed into an abstract spatial structure shows affinity to the architectural language of the late 20th century. Using the camera, the photographer deconstructed modern architectural form, suggesting a potential for different approaches to space and for developing new visions of architecture.

Josef Sudek

Untitled (Staircase), 1930s
The Museum of Fine Arts, Houston;
museum purchase with funds provided by
the Alice Pratt Brown Museum Fund

B Y T A

Arch. MIES VAN DER ROHE OBYTNÁ HALA VE VILE. BRNO

U M Ě N Í

REVUE PRO SOUČASNOU BYTOVOU KULTURU · ARCHITEKTURA
VNITŘNÍ ZAŘÍZENÍ · MALÍŘSTVÍ · PLASTIKA · UMĚLECKÝ
PRŮMYSL · RUČNÍ PRÁCE · STAROŽITNOSTI · VÝSTAVY · AUKCE

architecture
in print

[...] the promotion and advancement of [...] ideas cannot do without the effective help of the press; be it journals that architects created with great perseverance and not a small amount of sacrifice, without help from outside, and which they maintain at a high formal and informative level; be it books and booklets in which architects and theoreticians store the results of their fine artistic and scientific work [...]

K. Storch, "The Library and the Reading Room [Knihovna a čítárna]," 1940

architecture
in print

Buildings as complex spatial structures are constantly interpreted and reinterpreted in various media—drawings, paintings, models, photographs, and films. Images of modern buildings have been viewed, constructed, reproduced, and transmitted most frequently by means of photographs and their photomechanical reproduction. The primary vehicles of the transmission or distribution of these images were architectural exhibitions and architectural publications.

Emerging in the second half of the 19th century and published by professional organizations, architectural magazines and journals played a crucial role in architectural discourse.[174] Early architectural journals used wood-engravings and lithographs, but the advent of photomechanical reproduction in the last quarter of the 19th century gradually made photography the preferred medium for reproducing architecture as well as other art forms. This development resulted in the rise of a reprographic industry represented by new companies such as the Jan Štenc Graphic Enterprise in Prague that specialized in photographic and photomechanical reproductions of works of art and architecture.[175]

Štenc closely collaborated with the leading artists' association S.V.U. Mánes and its art monthly *Volné směry* [Free Directions] (1897–1949) and architectural journal *Styl* [Style] (1908–38). The Mánes architects adopted the late Art Nouveau style, also called *moderna* [modern style] style, which originated in the work of Otto Wagner with whom several important Czech architects studied in Vienna, including Jan Kotěra (who became an influential educator himself in Prague) and Pavel Janák. But the modern movement in architecture in the 1920s and 1930s was associated with a different organization called the Architects' Club, an association founded in Prague in 1913 by architects who graduated from the Czech Technical University in Prague and Brno, such as Oldřich Tyl and Ludvík Kysela. In 1922 the club started to publish the monthly *Stavba* [Construction] (1922–38) which was soon recognized as an international platform for the modern movement in architecture.[176] Karel Teige, who became its managing editor in 1923, broadened the narrow scope of a professional journal into an avantgarde publication which covered important art events and printed reproductions of works in other media, including photography. When the club organized an international series of lectures by pioneering figures of modern architecture, including Adolf Loos, Le Corbusier, and Jacobus Johannes Pieter Oud in Prague and Brno in 1924 and 1925, the text of their lectures appeared in *Stavba* in 1925 accompanied by a summary and an editorial written as a manifesto of the modern movement in architecture.[177] *Stavba's* international aspirations raised the benchmark for other architectural journals such as *Stavitel* [Builder] (1919–38), which was published by the Architects' Association (an organization of graduates of the College of Applied Arts and the Academy of Fine Arts in Prague) and which posted its own manifesto in 1926, signed by both Czech and international architects.[178] Another architectural journal was *Architekt SIA* [Architect SIA] (1927–44, 1946–51), which succeeded *Časopis československých architektů* [Journal of Czechoslovak Architects] (1922–26).

In Brno, which competed with Prague as a center of modern architecture, two architectural and design journals ran for a few years. *Bytová kultura* [Dwelling Culture] (1924–25), which had Adolf Loos, a Brno native, on its editorial board, was published by the architect Jan Vaněk,

STAVBA

FORUM

VI. № 8   1936

S   XXVI   4
I   1927

ARCHITEKT

DŮM ČESKOSLOVENSKÝCH INŽENÝRŮ

4
5

(XIII) 1932

letiště · les aéroports · flughäfe

G-AAGX

stavitel

měsíčník pro architekturu
revue mensuelle d'architecture
monatsheft für baukunst

žijeme

DISK

internacionální moderní revue
LE DISQUE, revue internationale d'avant-garde
DER DISKUS, internationale moderne Zeitschrift
Il DISCO, rivista internazionale d'avanguardia
ДИСК, интернациональная ревю
THE DISC, international review

PRAGUE — PARIS

NOVÉ UMĚNÍ · KINO · PROLETÁŘSKÁ KULTURA
REVOLUCE · SOUDOBÁ INTELEKTUELNÍ AKTIVITA
FILOSOFIE · SOCIOLOGIE · MARXISMUS · TECHNICKÁ
KULTURA · MODERNÍ ŽIVOT · UDÁLOSTI A OBRAZY
ZE SVĚTA · SLAVNOSTI · SPORT · CIRKUS · VARIÉTÉ
NOVÁ ESTETIKA

RED   5

měsíčník pro moderní kulturu

1928

JAROMÍR KREJCAR 1926

MEZINÁRODNÍ
SOUDOBÁ
ARCHITEKTURA

ODEON   6 Kč

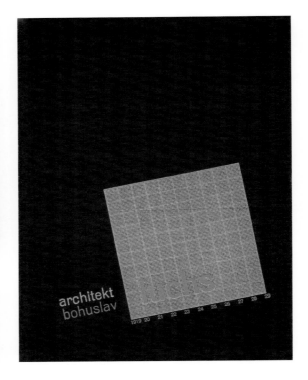

who was head of the furniture company UP Enterprises. It was followed by *Horizont* (1927–31) initiated by Jiří Kroha, which focused primarily on the works of Brno architects, dedicating its monothematic issues to the work of individual architects or to major projects such as the *Exhibition of Contemporary Culture in Czechoslovakia* in 1928. Svaz československého díla, an equivalent of the German Werkbund, published *Výtvarné snahy* [Plastic Endeavors] (1926–30), a monthly specialized in design and architecture. Among other journals which provided a platform for authors who were not associated with influential organizations were *Stavitelské listy* [Developers' Newsletter] (1904–42), *Stavební rádce* [Building Adviser] (1928–41), and *Kámen* [Stone] (1919–42). *Tchéco-Verre* [Czech Glass] (1934–37) was a journal specialized in glass production and use, especially in architecture, edited by Jaroslav Polívka who was a leading construction engineer and proponent of ferro-concrete, and glass lenses and bricks.

The Devětsil journals *Disk* (1923, 1925) and *Pásmo* [Zone] (1924–26), and *ReD* (Review of Devětsil, 1927–31) and the anthologies *Devětsil* (1922), *Život: Sborník nové krásy* [Life; Anthology of the New Beauty] (1922) and *Fronta* [Front] (1927) closely followed developments on the international avant-garde scene, including architecture. Among general art magazines, *Forum* (1931–38) covered architecture most extensively. Published in Bratislava, this monthly was also interesting for its multilingual character and focus on Central Europe. The review *Musaion* (1929–31) published by the Aventinum publishing house in Prague gave considerable space to the polemic between Karel Teige and Le Corbusier regarding the Swiss architect's project of the Mundaneum.[179] Družstevní práce, a cooperative publishing house that also produced objects of everyday use and promoted modern design, published the magazines *Panorama* (1922–38) and *Žijeme* [We Live] (1931–32), later renamed *Magazin DP* (1933–37) which focused on various aspects of modern lifestyle and popularized architecture as its important element and brought out numerous pictures by Josef Sudek, including some of his architectural photographs. *Byt a umění* [Dwelling and Art] (1930–32) focused on interior design, but in some cases also publicized important architectural realizations such as Villa Tugendhat in Brno by Ludwig Mies van der Rohe, which, curiously, did not receive attention in other Czech architectural journals. Using photographs to document the most recent architectural realizations as an expression of the modern age, pictorial magazines of general interest such as *Pestrý týden* [Varied Week], *Světozor* [World View], *Letem světem* [Across the World], *Domov a svět* [Home and Abroad], *Gentleman*, and *Eva* presented modern architecture in a similar way.

Exhibition catalogues that accompanied architectural exhibitions were another important form of presentation used in proselytizing for the modern movement. Both exhibitions and their catalogs were designed by prominent architects and designers, such as Zdeněk Rossmann (the catalogs for the exhibitions *Nový dům* [New House] and *Výstava stavebnictví a bydlení* [Exhibition of Construction Industry and Housing] in Brno in 1928 and 1932), Václav Roštlapil (the *Výstava soudobé kultury v Československu* [Exhibition of Contemporary Culture in Czechoslovakia] catalog which included a section on architecture and urban planning), Ladislav Sutnar who designed exhibitions and catalogs of Czech architecture and design exhibitions in foreign countries such as Romania (1930), Sweden (1931), and Switzerland (1931), and the exhibition catalog of the Baba Settlement in Prague (1932).

The production of architectural exhibitions and books was closely interconnected. For instance, Karel Teige's volumes *Mezinárodní soudobá architektura: sborník* [International Contemporary Architecture: An Anthology] (1929) and *Moderní architektura v Československu* [Modern Architecture in Czechoslovakia] (1930) followed soon after the traveling exhibition of the new architecture organized by the German Werkbund, which took place in Prague in 1929 and

o bydlení

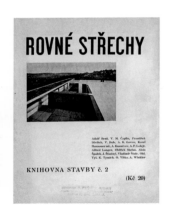

Ladislav Sutnar
Cover of *O bydlení* [On Housing], 1932
Private collection

Josef Hesoun
Cover of *Zařízení a úprava moderní
kanceláře a obchodu* [Modern Office and
Store Furnishing and Design] by K. Burian
and J. Hesoun, 1930
Private collection

Vojtěch Krch
Cover of *Okno: součást budovy a obytné
místnosti* [The Window: A Building and
Dwelling Component], 1935
Private collection

Designer unknown
Cover of *Architektura průmyslových staveb*
[The Architecture of Industrial Buildings]
by Otakar Štěpánek, 1936
Private collection

Ladislav Sutnar (?)
Cover of *Město a upravovací plán* [City and
Regulating Plan], 1932
Private collection

Designer unknown
Cover of *Rovné střechy* [Flat Roofs] by Karel
Hannauer, 1929
Private collection

Ladislav Sutnar
Cover of *Obytný dům dneška* [Contemporary
Dwelling] by Jan E. Koula, 1931
Private collection

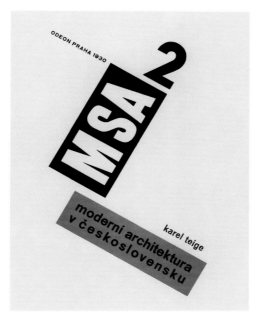
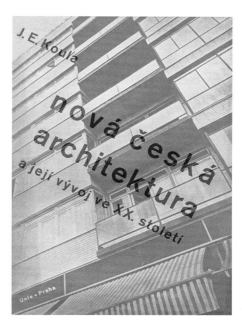

Jaromír Krejcar

Cover of *L'architecture contemporaine
en Tchécoslovaquie,* 1928
Private collection

Karel Teige

Cover of *Moderní architektura
v Československu* [Modern Architecture
in Czechoslovakia], 1930
Private collection

Jan E. Koula

Cover of *Nová česká architektura a její
vývoj ve XX. století* [New Czech
Architecture and Its Evolution in the
Twentieth Century], 1940
Private collection

was complemented with a section on Czech modern architecture.[180] Similarly, the first historical account of Czech modern architecture, the book *Nová česká architektura a její vývoj ve
XX. století* [New Czech Architecture and Its Evolution in the 20th century] by Jan E. Koula
appeared in the same year as the exhibition *Za novou architekturu* [In Praise of the New Archi-
tecture] (1940). The exhibition catalog consisted primarily of a checklist and short introductions
to individual sections, but did not include any illustrations as it announced a large publication on
the subject which, however, did not materialize.[181]

Architectural publications harnessed the media of photography and typography to trans-
mit the modern movement's ideas and images as well as to promote the work of architects.
Bohuslav Fuchs was one of the architects who, very early on, understood the significance of
publicity for the reception of modern architecture and architectural practice. He collaborated
with leading critics, designers and photographers while publishing brochures on his realizations
and projects.[182] His monograph (1930) edited and designed by Zdeněk Rossmann was an example of an effective presentation which integrated new architecture, photography, and typography into a visual and conceptual unity.

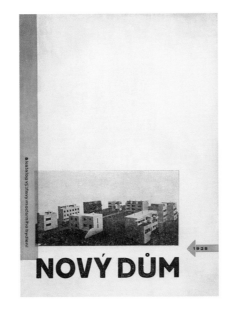

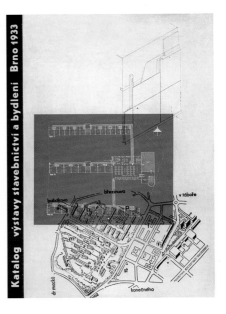

Ladislav Sutnar
Cover of *Tjeckoslovakisk arkitektur och konstindustri*, 1931
Private collection

Zdeněk Rossmann
Cover of *Nový dům; katalog výstavy moderního bydlení v Brně* [The New House; Catalog of the Exhibition of Modern Housing in Brno], 1928
Private collection

Zdeněk Rossmann
Cover of *Katalog výstavy stavebnictví a bydlení v Brně* [Catalog of the Exhibition of Construction Industry and Housing in Brno], 1933
Private collection

PAS (Karel Janů, Jiří Štursa, Jiří Voženílek)
Poster for *Výstava stavebnictví a bydlení v Praze* [Exhibition of Construction Industry and Housing in Prague], 1932
Private collection

Václav Roštlapil
Cover of *Výstava soudobé kultury v ČSR* [Exhibition of Contemporary Culture in Czechoslovakia], 1928
Private collection

Ladislav Sutnar
Cover of *Výstava bydlení; Stavba osady Baba* [Exhibition of Housing; the Baba Settlement Development], 1932
Private collection

Designer unknown
Advertising brochure, 1930s
Private collection

Designer unknown
Advertising brochure, 1930s
Private collection

Ladislav Sutnar (?)
Advertising brochure, 1930s
Private collection

Designer unknown
Advertising brochure, 1930s
Private collection

In his architectural publications, Karel Teige pursued a critical agenda that emphasized the social and political underpinnings of architectural production, identifying architecture with science, not art. The subject of housing, as Teige's book *Nejmenší byt* [Minimum Dwelling] (1932) demonstrated, was central to his concerns. In this respect, Teige's photomontage cover for the book is emblematic in its juxtaposition of a traditional apartment building with a free-standing building endowed with a great number of balconies. Complemented by a cut-out from the classified real estate section of a newspaper, the juxtaposition summarizes Teige's argument that the great demand for affordable housing can be met only by replacing the traditional types of housing such as the closed blocks of apartment buildings with open-structure buildings, and by replacing vagaries of the market with rational planning. The fact that the modern building reproduced in the montage happened to be a sanatorium (notably the sanatorium at Trenčianske Teplice designed by Krejcar) suggests that Teige saw the family and the family house replaced with collective living and housing in the future.[183]

Sutnar's cover for the publication *Nejmenší dům* [Minimum Family House] (1931), which presented the awarded projects in a competition for low-income houses, showed a very different approach. Sutnar put a premium on visual forms rather than on ideological concepts. The red square he used as the central motif referred to the language of architectural and graphic design, notably to the logo of Max Burchartz's publication on graphic design *Buntquadrat* (1924–25) as well as to Farkas Molnár's cover for the first volume of Bauhausbücher, *Internationale Architektur* (1925) by Walter Gropius, which was reminiscent of Molnár's influential *Red Cube* project for a house.[184] If Sutnar's red square refers to the house, then the grid on his cover seems to be derived from the grid of tiles on the house roof-top in the photograph by Josef Sudek that Sutnar used for the cover of the book *Obytný dům dneška* [The Contemporary Dwelling] (1931) by Jan E. Koula. This would explain the feeling of openness communicated by Sutnar's montage, contrasting with Teige's message of sociopolitical determinism. In Sutnar's cover, the grid is not rendered as a confined system but as a platform which opens up new possibilities.

The popularization of modern architecture was closely associated with the use of media that reached a mass audience, such as illustrated magazines (weeklies or monthlies), advertising and postcards in which photography had the central role. Illustrated magazines often reproduced photographs of new buildings and brought out articles on modern architecture. This theme also often appeared in advertising as modern architecture advanced new building methods and materials which provided the construction industry with new incentives and opportunities. Advertisers exploited modern photography and typography to market their products in special advertising brochures devoted to individual construction components (including doors and windows), new building materials (such as glass brick) and complete building prototypes. For instance, the Vítkovice Iron Company advertised three prefabricated types of steel skeleton family houses in a brochure: its cover featured a quintessential image of the modern family house with a flat roof, horizontal windows, and a white façade free of decoration.

Postcards contributed to the distribution of photographs of modern architecture in a special personal way, since they were part of interpersonal communication. The image of modern architecture represented a universal vision independent of a particular place, but postcards recycled this image in the domain of everyday life, returning it back to the specificity of history, individual as well as collective.

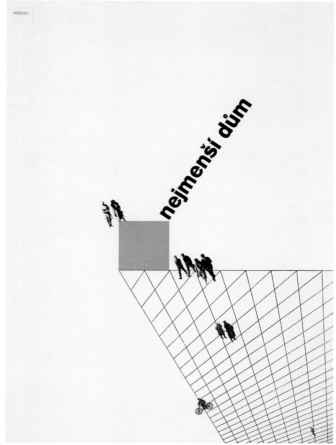

Karel Teige

Cover of *Nejmenší byt* [Minimum Dwelling],
1932
Private collection

Ladislav Sutnar

Cover of *Nejmenší dům* [Minimum Family
House], 1931
Private collection

n o t e s

1. Quoted after the first English translation by Frederick Etchells in *Towards a New Architecture*. London: John Rodker, 1927.

2. See Paul V. Turner, *The Education of Le Corbusier*. New York: Garland Publishing, 1977.

3. See Beatriz Colomina, *Le Corbusier and Photography*. Cambridge, Mass.: Harvard University Press, 1987.

4. František Čermák, "Největší výstava fotografických zvětšenin." *Foto-Noviny*, No. 21 (October 1940), pp. 18–20.

5. Josef Sudek, *Fotografie*. Praha: SNKLHU, 1956, il. nos. 60, 61.

6. See Richard Pare, *Architecture and Photography, 1839–1940*. Cambridge, Mass.: The MIT Press, 1982. This book, which served as an exhibition catalog, includes photographs of modern architecture from the 1920s and 1930s.

7. See Jürgen E. Müller, *Intermedialität. Formen moderner kultureller Kommunikation*. Münster: 1996. Jörg Helbich, ed., *Intermedialität. Theorie und Praxis eines interdisziplinären Forschungsgebiets*. Berlin: Erich Schmidt Verlag, 1998.

8. See Kenneth Frampton, "A Modernity Worthy of the Name: Notes on the Czech Architectural Avant-Garde." In: *The Artistic Avant-Garde in Czechoslovakia 1918–1938*. Jaroslav Anděl, ed. Valencia: IVAM, pp. 213–231.

9. Jaroslav Anděl, "Modernism, the Avant-Garde, and Photography." *Czech Modernism 1900–1945*. Jaroslav Anděl and Anne W. Tucker, eds. Boston; Houston: The Museum of Fine Arts, Houston; Bullfinch Press, 1989, pp. 87–113.

10. Walter Benjamin, "Paris, Capital of the Nineteenth Century." In: Walter Benjamin, *Reflections*. New York/London: 1978, p. 161. See also Walter Benjamin, *The Arcades Project*. Cambridge, Mass.: Harvard University Press, 2002. For a discussion of the *Arcades project*, see Susan Buck-Morss, *The Dialectics of Seeing. Walter Benjamin and the Arcades Projects*. Cambridge, Mass.: The MIT Press, 1994.

11. See *Art into Life: Russian Constructivism 1914–1932*. Richard Andrews and Milena Kalinovska, eds. New York: Rizzoli, 1990. For additional discussion, see Christina Lodder, *Russian Constructivism*. New Haven and London: Yale University Press, 1983.

12. Besides Teige's article "Foto Kino Film," other texts examined the subject of cinema or included passages on it, including a quote by Georg Grosz, and the articles by Jindřich Honzl ("Nestavte divadla [Do not build theaters]"), Jean Epstein ("Kino"), Louis Delluc ("Dav před kinoplátnem [Crowd in Front of the Screen]"). *Život*, vol. 2 (Prague: Výtvarný odbor Umělecké besedy, 1922), pp. 153–168; 64; 104–108; 143–147; 148–152.

13. Karel Teige, "Foto kino film." *Život*, vol. 2 (1922), p. 156.

14. Jaromír Krejcar, "Made in America." *Život*, vol. 2 (1922), p. 195.

15. These pictures appeared in *L'Esprit nouveau* in 1921 (no. 10, p. 1141), illustrating one of Le Corbusier's articles on the new architecture which were reprinted in his book *Vers une architecture*. Paris: Editions Crès, 1923, p. 106.

16. For a discussion of this relation, see Jaroslav Anděl, "Sen o Devětsilu." *Umění*, vol. 35 (1987), no. 1, pp. 50–53.

17. Karel Teige, "Naše základna a naše cesta. Konstruktivismus a poetismus [Our Base and Our Path. Constructivism and Poetism]." *Pásmo*, vol. 1 (1924), no. 3, pp. 1–2.

18. Karel Teige, "Obrazy [Pictures]." *Veraikon*, vol. 10 (1924), nos. 3–5, pp. 34–40.

19. Josef Čapek's writings, especially the book *Nejskromnější umění* [The Most Modest Art] (Prague: Aventinum, 1920), had a great impact on the Devětsil artists and paved the way for their celebration of popular art.

20. See Lodder, op. cit., p. 72.

21. *Stavba*, vol. 3 (1924–25), no. 12, p. 221. For a discussion of this genre in Czech photography, see Jan Hozák and Pavel Scheufler, *Člověk a technika v české fotografii do roku 1914*. Roztoky u Prahy: Středočeské muzeum, 1987. For additional discussion, see *Průmysl a technika v novodobé české kultuře. Sborník symposia v Plzni 14. – 16. 3. 1985*. Praha: Ústav teorie a dějin umění Československé akademie věd, 1988.

22. The quote comes from the essay "On the Present Condition and Prospects of Architecture," which was published in 1886. Reprinted in *Architecture and Society. Selected essays of Henry van Brunt*, ed. W. A. Coles. Cambridge, Mass.: 1969, p. 165. Quoted after Nikolaus Pevsner, *A History of Building Types*. Princeton: Princeton University Press, 1979, p. 9.

23. *Život*, vol. 2 (1922), p. 45. It is interesting that the commentary (written most probably by Karel Teige) that accompanied the two illustrations was critical of Tatlin's Tower for its lack of functionalism and for "the fever of machinistic élan."

24. See Anna Fárová, "Film und Foto und die Tschechoslowakei." In: *Film und Foto der zwanziger Jahre. Eine Betrachtung der internationalen Werkbundausstellung "Film und Foto" 1929*. Ute Eskildsen and Jan-Christoph Horak, eds. Stuttgart: Verlag Gerd Hatje, 1979, pp. 180–182.

25. Jaroslav Fragner, "Nemocniční pavilon [Hospital Pavilion]." *Stavba*, vol. 3, 1924–25, pp. 48–49.

26. "Zásady nové architektury [Tenets of the New Architecture]." *Stavba*, vol. 3 (1924–25), no. 9, pp. 153–158.

27. Karel Honzík, *Ze života avantgardy*. Prague: Československý spisovatel, 1963, pp. 185–188.

28. Jan Kučera, "Film a stavba [Cinema and Construction]." *Volné směry*, vol. 30 (1933–34), no. 2, pp. 40–42.

29. See Jan Svoboda, "Začátky Jana Kučery a okruh devětsilské avantgardy." *Umění*, vol. 35 (1987), no. 2, pp. 158–166.

30. *Výstava Za novou architekturu*, Praha: Uměleckoprůmyslové muzeum, 1940, p. 11.

31. Ibid.

32. Karel Teige, "Le Corbusier v Praze [Le Corbusier in Prague]." *Rozpravy Aventina*, vol. 4 (1928–29), p. 31–32.

33. See Rostislav Švácha, "Definitivní projekt, jeho autorství." Miroslav Masák, Rostislav Švácha, and Jindřich Vybíral, *Veletržní palác v Praze*. Praha: Národní galerie, 1996, pp. 16–21.

34. See *Brno: Přehled historického, hospodářského, sociálního a stavebního rozvoje* [Brno: A Survey of Historical, Economical, Social and Architectural Development]. Brno: 1935. For additional discussion, see *O nové Brno. Brněnská architektura 1919–1939*. Zdeněk Kudělka and Jindřich Chatrný, eds. Brno: Muzeum města Brna, 2000. *The Brno Functionalists*. Vladimír Šlapeta, ed. Helsinki: Finnish Museum of Architecture, 1983.

35. See the chapter "Family Houses" in this book. *The New House Exhibition* was the subject of the publication *Nový dům. Katalog výstavy moderního bydlení* [The New House. Catalog of the Exhibition of Modern Housing]. Bedřich Václavek and Zdeněk Rossmann, eds. Brno: 1928.

36. See *O nové Brno. Brněnská architektura 1919–1939*. Zdeněk Kudělka and Jindřich Chatrný, eds. Brno: Muzeum města Brna, 2000.

37. See Jiří Kroha, "Jak jsem budoval expozici moderní vědy [How I built the exposition of modern science]." *Horizont*, nos. 14–16, 1928, pp. 63–64.

38. For Karel Teige's criticism of Kroha's design, see Karel Teige, "Výtvarné umění na výstavě soudobé kultury [Fine Arts at the Exhibition of Contemporary Culture]." *Stavba*, vol. 7 (1928–29), no. 3, p. 46.

39. Přerov, Písek, Vodňany, České Budějovice, Ostrava, Liberec, and Pilsen were among other towns that held regional trade fairs.

40. See Walter Benjamin, *The Arcades Project*. Cambridge, Mass.: Harvard University Press, 2002.

41. Kenneth Frampton, op. cit., p. 226.

42. See Philip G. Norde, *Paris Shopkeepers and the Politics of Resentment*. Princeton: Princeton University Press, 1986.

43. See Geoffrey Crossick and Serge Jaumain, "The World of the Department Store: Distribution, Culture and Social Change." *Cathedral of Consumption. The European Department Store, 1850–1939*. Geoffrey Crossick and Serge Jaumain, eds. Aldershot: Ashgate, 1999, pp. 1–45.

44. See Rosalind Williams, *Dream Worlds. Mass Consumption in Late-Nineteenth Century France*. Berkeley: University of California, 1982.

45. Émile Zola explored the theme of the department store in his novel *Au Bonheur des Dames* (1883).

46. See Geoffrey Crossick and Serge Jaumain, op. cit.

47. See Philip G. Norde, op. cit.

48. See Geoffrey Crossick and Serge Jaumain, op. cit.

49. See Michael Miller, *The Bon Marché. Bourgeois Culture and the Department Store 1869–1920*. Princeton: Princeton University Press, 1981.

50. See Geoffrey Crossick and Serge Jaumain, op. cit. For additional discussion, see Nikolaus Pevsner, op. cit.

51. Josef Kittrich and Josef Hrubý, "Obchodní dům Bílá labuť [The Bílá Labuť Department Store]." *Stavba*, vol. 14 (1937–38), no. 5, p. 91. A passage from this article appeared in *Czech Functionalism 1918–1938*, London: Architectural Association, 1987, p. 143.

52. See Michael Miller, op. cit. and Geoffrey Crossick and Serge Jaumain, op. cit.

53. *Volné směry*, vol. 29 (1931–32), no. 4, pp. 98–99.

54. Alluding to Freudian symbolism, Funke's photograph of a smokestack is from the *Time Persists* series (1930–32).

55. For illustration, see Rumjana Dačeva et al., *Karel Teige: Surrealistické koláže, 1935–1951*. Praha: Středoevropská galerie a nakladatelství, 1994, p. 42.

56. See note 21.

57. *Výstava Za novou architekturu*, p. 12.

58. "Architect Le Corbusier on Zlín." *Zlín: The Town of Activity*. Zlín: Baťa Works, 1938, p. 47.

59. See "Zlín in a Nutshell." *Zlín: The Town of Activity*, p. 11. For additional discussion of Baťa's global expansion, see Otakar Nový, *Česká architektonická avantgarda*. Praha: Prostor, 1998. Pavel Novák, *Zlínská architektura 1900–1950*. Zlín: 1993.

60. For Tomáš Baťa's views on architecture, see Tomáš Baťa, "Technický a organizační pokrok ve výrobě [Technical and Organizational Progress in Production]." *Stavitel*, vol. 6 (1924–25), nos. 4–5, pp. 49–56.

61. Op. cit. For Baťa's praise of the American economy and management style, see Tomáš Baťa, op. cit., pp. 53, 56.

62. František L. Gahura, "How Zlín was built." *Stavitel*, vol. 14 (1933–34), nos. 10–12, p. 136. This issue was also published separately under the title *Urbanismus a architektura Závodů Baťa a. s. ve Zlíně*. Josef Setnička, ed. Praha: Sdružení architektů, 1934, p. 6.

63. For a discussion of garden cities, see Stanley Buder, *Visionaries & Planners. The Garden City Movement and the Modern Community*. New York: Oxford University Press, 2002.

64. František L. Gahura, op. cit.

65. Quoted in: Pavel Halík, "Zlín." *The Cultural Phenomenon of Functionalism*. Zlín: SGZ, 1996, p. 26.

66. Vladimír Karfík, *Architekt si spomína*. Bratislava: Spolok architektov Slovenska, 1993, p. 125. For Karfík's description in English, see *Czech Functionalism 1918–1938*, p. 145.

67. This information was provided by Pavel Hrdlička, one of the cameramen of the Baťa film studios.

68. Vladimír Karfík, op. cit., p. 130. For a description of the Baťa schools, see Jaromír Hradil, "Baťovy školy ve Zlíně [Baťa's School in Zlín]." *Stavitel*, vol. 8 (1926–27), pp. 153–156.

69. See Eduard Staša, *Kronika moderní architektury Gottwaldova*. Prague: Svaz českých architektů, 1985, unpaginated.

70. For a discussion of Le Corbusier's collaboration with Baťa, see Vladimír Karfík, op. cit., pp. 118–123.

71. See Rostislav Švácha, "Modernost bez avantgardy." In: *The Cultural Phenomenon of Functionalism*. Zlín: SGZ, 1996, pp. 19–24.

72. See Rostislav Švácha, op. cit.

73. František L. Gahura, "Poměry ve stavbě obydlí a měst za 40 let [Conditions in Housing and City Construction in 40 Years]." *Stavitel*, vol. 14 (1933–34), nos. 10–12, pp. 138–139.

74. Ibid., p. 139.

75. Eduard Staša, op. cit., (unpaginated).

76. Siegfried Giedion made this comment with respect to Le Corbusier's houses in Pessac in 1928. See *Cinema and Architecture*. François Penz and Maureen Thomas, eds. London, British Film Institute, 1997. For additional discussion of the subject, see T*he Cinematic City*. David B. Clarke, ed. New York: Routledge, 1995.

77. See Beatriz Colomina, *Privacy and Publicity: Modern Architecture as Mass Media*. Cambridge, Mass.: MIT Press, 1994. For additional discussion, see M. Christian Boyer, "Le Corbusier's Cinematic Architecture." www.restesurbain.sal.qc.ca/files/boyer.htm

78. See Beatriz Colomina, op. cit. For additional discussion, see M. Christian Boyer, *Cybercities*. New York: Princeton Architectural Press, 1996.

79. Edwin Heathcote, *Cinema Builders*. San Francisco: J. Wiley, 2001.

80. *Stavba*, vol. 3 (1924–25), no. 11, p. 193. Koula's design also appeared in the book *Film* by Karel Teige. Prague: Petr, 1925, pp. 76–77.

81. Králík's movie theater has not been preserved in its original condition.

82. For a description of Zlín's movie theaters, see Václav Kaplický, "Půl dne v království Baťově [Half a Day in the Baťa Kingdom]. *Žijeme 1932*, vol. 2 (1932), nos. 3–4, pp. 79–82. For a discussion of the Baťa film studios, see Petr Novotný, "Kudlov Barn." In: *The Cultural Phenomenon of Functionalism*. Zlín: Státní galerie umění, 1995, pp. 109–115.

83. Arne Hošek, "Adaptace sálu pro kino Alfa v Moravské Ostravě [Space Adaptation for the Alfa Movie Theater in Moravská Ostrava]." *Architekt*, vol. 1 (1939), p. 272. Hošek published several articles on acoustics and a couple of texts on cinema, including "Stavební akustika [Building Acoustics]," *Stavba*, vol. 9 (1930–31), p. 179; and "Kompozice, umění, film a divadlo [Composition, Art, Cinema, and Theater]," *Magazin Družstevní práce*, vol. 1 (1933–34), pp. 277–279. For a discussion of Hošek's work and bibliography, see *Arne Hošek. Souvislost barev a tónů*. Hana Rousová, ed. Praha: GHMP, 1991. Josef Kittrich was another architect who wrote on acoustics and architecture. See Josef Kittrich, "Organisace akustického prostoru." *Stavba*, vol. 11 (1932–33), no. 10, pp. 145–151.

84. Miroslav Kouřil and Emil F. Burian, *Divadlo práce. Studie divadelního prostoru* [The Theater of Work. A Study of Theatrical Space]. Prague: Jaroslav Kohoutek, 1938. For a discussion of the use of photography and film in Czech theater, see Vladimír Birgus, "Photography in the Czech Avant-Garde Theater." *Czech Photographic Avant-Garde 1918–1948*. Vladimír Birgus, ed. Cambridge, Mass.: The MIT Press, 2003, pp. 273–280.

85. See the brochure *Jarní festival D37, 6. květen–15. květen, 1937* [Spring Festival D37, May 6–May 15, 1937]. Prague: D37, 1937.

86. See Jaroslav Anděl, "Artists as Filmmakers." *Czech Modernism 1900–1945*. Jaroslav Anděl and Anne W. Tucker, eds. Houston: The Museum of Fine Arts, 1989, pp. 165–167.

87. See Jiří Zemánek, "In the Sign of the Stars – The Aviators' Monument." *Zdeněk Pešánek 1896–1965*. Jiří Zemánek, ed. Prague: Národní galerie, 1998, pp. 369–382. For a discussion of Le Corbusier's project, see Zdeněk Lukeš, "Vladimír Karfík vypráví." *Revolver Revue*, no. 42 (January 2000), pp. 272–310.

88. Jiří Zemánek, "A City of Lights. The Beginning of Zdeněk Pešánek's Work with the Electricity Companies of the City of Prague." *Zdeněk Pešánek 1896–1965*. Jiří Zemánek, ed. Prague: Národní galerie, 1998, pp. 385–402.

89. Jaroslav Anděl, "Artists as Filmmakers." Op. cit., p. 170. For additional discussion, see Jiří Zemánek, op. cit., pp. 395.

90. See Zdeněk Lukeš, "Architekt Otto Klein a dynamický expresionismus v české architektuře." Umění a řemesla, vol. 30, no. 2, 1988, p. 70. An airplane and airplane engines were shown at the Baťa Memorial in Zlín. Pictures of airplane engines accompanied the article "Motory [Engines]" by Vilém Santholzer in Pásmo, vol. 1 (1924), no. 9, p. 2. Photographs of an airplane as a component of an exhibition design, notably of Sutnar's and Fuchs's design of the exhibition in Stockholm in 1931, appeared in Stavba, vol. 10 (1931–32), no. 6, p. 99, and in Žijeme 1931, vol. 1 (1931), no. 9, p. 287.

91. See Thomas Baťa, "Aviation in Zlín." Zlín. The Town of Activity. Zlín: Baťa Works, 1938, p. 24. "Aviation." Ibid., p. 25.

92. Stavba and Stavitel, two leading architectural journals that promoted the modern movement, often publicized the theme of aviation. For instance, Stavitel dedicated a special issue to the subject in 1932 (vol. 13, nos. 4–5).

93. See note 91.

94. See Aaron Scharf, Art and Photography. London: Penguin, 1974, pp. 176, 294–295, 352, 374.

95. For a discussion of artificialism see, Lenka Bydžovská and Karel Srp, Štyrský, Toyen. Artificialismus 1926–1931. Prague; Pardubice: GHMP; OVG, 1992.

96. Foto-Auge. Jan Tschichold and Franz Roh, eds. Stuttgart: Franz Wedekind, 1929.

97. See Jill Lever, "Architectural Drawing." The Dictionary of Art. Jane Turner, ed. New York: Grove's Dictionaries, 1996, vol. 2, pp. 333–334.

98. One of these parallels can be seen in the popularity of axonometry among proponents of the new architecture and the popularity of the bird's-eye view among avant-garde photographers.

99. Výstava Za novou architekturu, p. 11.

100. Op. cit., p. 43. Benš published an article on the office building in Stavitel in 1927, shortly after he won the competition for the Prague Electricty Board Building. "Moderní kancelářská budova [The Modern Office Building]," Stavitel, vol. 8 (1926–27), pp. 80–84.

101. Ústřední budova Elektrických podniků hlavního města Prahy. Praha: Elektrické podniky hl. m. Prahy, 1935. Josef Havlíček and Karel Honzík, Návrh Paláce všeobecného pensijního ústavu v Praze. Praha: Odeon, 1930.

102. Adolf Benš and Josef Kříž, "Sociální předpoklady plánů a architektury [Social Conditions for Projects and Architecture]." Ústřední budova Elektrických podniků hlavního města Prahy. Praha: Elektrické podniky hlavního města Prahy, 1935, p. 23.

103. Ibid., p. 24.

104. For a contemporary discussion of lighting, see Stavba, vol. 12 (1933–34), no. 11.

105. See Karel Honzík, Ze života avantgardy. Prague: Československý spisovatel, 1963, pp. 160–162.

106. See "Klub za novu Prahu ustaven dne 10. 6. 1924." Stavba, vol. 3 (1924–25), p. 43. This manifesto was against, among other things, the "superstition of genius loci" and the "preservation of the city character."

107. Josef Havlíček and Emanuel Hruška, Cestou k novému Žižkovu [On the Way to the New Žižkov]. Prague: Petr, 1940.

108. Říha's building also represents an important example of the steel skeleton construction.

109. Kenneth Frampton, op. cit., p. 226.

110. See Karel Teige: Práce Jaromíra Krejcara. Praha: Petr, 1933, p. 75.

111. Bohuslav Fuchs, Josef Polášek, "Stavba učiliště pro ženská povolání Vesna [The Construction of the Vesna Vocational School for Women]." Stavitel, vol. 11 (1929–30), no. 12, p. 150.

112. Iba Eberhardová, "Hygiena a pohyb [Hygienics and Movement]." Výroční zpráva Masarykova městského učitelského ústavu pro odborné školy ženských povolání Vesna v Brně 1931–32, Brno: 1932, p. 3.

113. František Kalivoda, "Neuzeitliche Schulbauten in Brünn." Forum, vol. 7, 1937, pp. 153–164. The school as a building type was the subject of several articles and special issues of Stavba and Stavitel in the 1920s and 1930s, including Vladimír Stříbrný, "Nové vlivy ve stavbě škol [New Influences in the Construction of Schools]." Stavba, vol. 9 (1930–31), no. 9, pp. 141–147; Josef Polášek, "Nové směry ve stavbě škol [New Directions in the Construction of Schools]." Stavitel, vol. 13 (1931–32), pp. 121–132; Oldřich Starý, "Moderní školy [Modern Schools]." Žijeme 1932, vol. 2 (1932), pp. 83–87; Václav Kolátor, "Naše školství a naše školy [Our Education System and Our Schools]." Stavba, vol. 14 (1935–36), no. 6, pp. 93–99.

114. František Kalivoda, op. cit., pp. 153, 155.

115. František Kalivoda, ibid., p. 155.

116. For a discussion of the Lebensreform movement in different fields, see Die Lebensreform. Entwürfe zur Neue Gestaltung von Kunst und Leben. Kai Buchholz, Rita Latocha, and Klaus Wolbert, eds. Darmstadt: Verlag Häuser, 2001, 2 vols.

117. Bohuslav Fuchs, Masarykův studentský domov, Brno [Bohuslav Fuchs, The Masaryk Student Dormitory, Brno]. Brno: Fuchs, 1930.

118. Iba Eberhardová, op. cit., p. 4.

119. See "Soutěž na francouzské školy v Praze XIX [The Competition for the French Schools in Prague XIX]." Stavba, vol. 10 (1931–32), no. 6, pp. 96–98. An excerpt from the article reprinted in English in Czech Functionalism 1918–1938, p. 95.

120. František Čermák and Gustav Paul, "Dnešní výstavba nemocnic [Hospital Construction Today]." Stavba, vol. 10 (1931–32), no. 5, pp. 69–74. Like schools, hospitals and sanatoriums were often written about in architectural journals in the 1920s and 1930s. Stavba dedicated several special issues to this subject, including two issues (nos. 5 and 10) in 1932.

121. Karel Teige, Práce Jaromíra Krejcara [The Work of Jaromír Krejcar]. Praha: Petr, 1933, p. 75.

122. See Klaus Wolbert, ed., op. cit.

123. Karel Teige, op. cit., p. 76.

124. Vladislav Vančura, Rozmarné léto [Quirky Summer]. Praha: Družstevní práce, 1926, pp. 11–12.

125. For illustration, see The Artistic Avant-Garde in Czechoslovakia 1918–1938. Jaroslav Anděl, ed. Valencia: IVAM Centre Julio Gonzalez, 1993, p. 72.

126. Karel Teige, op. cit., p. 75.

127. Anna Fárová, op. cit., p. 180.

128. Pestrý týden, Letem světem, Eva, Domov a svět, Světozor a Ahoj na neděli were among the most popular pictorial magazines.

129. Stavba, vol. 9 (1930–31), no. 10, p. 167.

130. Reproduced in: Karel Srp, Karel Teige. Prague: Torst, 2002, il. no. 41.

131. Artur Longen, "Vodní sporty [Water Sports]." Domov a svět, vol. 3 (1929), no. 26, p. 402.

132. Karel Honzík, Ze života avantgardy. Praha: Československý spisovatel, 1963, pp. 54–55.

133. Karel Honzík, op. cit., p. 54. For a discussion of the character of Prague cafés, see Jan E. Koula, "Nové pražské kavárny [New Prague Cafés]." Magazin Družstevní práce, vol. 1 (1933–34), no. 11, pp. 267–269.

134. Helmut Kreuzer, Die Bohème. Beiträge zu ihrer Beschreibung. Stuttgart: Metzler, 1968, p. 205. For additional discussion of the social significance of the café, see Albrecht Peter, Kaffee. Zur Sozialgeschichte eines Getränkes. Braunschweig, 1980; and Ulla Heise, Kaffee und Kaffeehaus. Eine Kulturgeschichte. Hildesheim; Zürich; New York: Olms Presse, 1987.

135. Karel Honzík, op. cit., p. 55.

136. Ibid., p. 59.

137. Henry Russell Hitchcock and Philip Johnson, The International Style: Architecture since 1922. New York: Norton, 1932 (most recently reprinted in 1996).

138. See Lenka Krčálová, "K historii a autorství paláce Morava." Sborník prací Filozofické fakulty brněnské univerzity, vols. 39–41. Brno: 1990–92, pp. 149–162. For a discussion of the Morava Building in the context of the late 20th century, see Charles Jencks and Silver Nathan, Adhocism. The Case of Improvisation. New York: Doubleday, 1972.

139. According to Pavel Hrdlička, it was Kolda who later commissioned Sudek to take pictures of Zlín.

140. The flyer included texts in four languages, Czech, German, French, and English.

141. For illustrations, see *Czech Photographic Avant-garde 1918–1948*, Vladimír Birgus, ed. Cambridge, Mass.: The MIT Press, 2002, pp. 128–129.

142. Oldřich Starý, "Proč rodinný dům [Why the Family House]." *Výstava bydlení; Stavba osady Baba*. Praha: Svaz československého díla, 1932, p. 6.

143. Ibid., p. 7.

144. See Jan Sedlák, "Kolonie Nový dům v Brně." *Zprávy památkové péče*, vol. 52 (1992), no. 2, p. 9.

145. *Výstava bydlení. Osada Baba. Praha 1931.* [The Housing Exhibition. The Baba Settlement. Prague 1931]. Prague: Výstavní výbor při Svazu Československého díla, 1931. Advertising leaflet.

146. *Výstava bydlení. Osada Baba. Praha 1931. Projekt vybudování výstavy bydlení v Praze XIX. Svaz Československého díla* [The Housing Exhibition. The Baba Settlement. Prague 1931. The Project of a Housing Exhibition in Prague XIX. The Czechoslovak Werkbund]. Advertising leaflet.

147. Ibid.

148. "Levá fronta." *ReD*, vol. 3 (1929), p. 48.

149. See Adolf Benš, "Výstava proletářského bydlení [The Exhibition of Proletarian Housing]." *Stavitel*, vol. 12 (1930–31), no. 7, pp. 101–06; and "Výstava proletářského bydlení [The Exhibition of Proletarian Housing]." *Stavba*, vol. 10 (1931–32), pp. 49–50.

150. Karel Teige, *Moderní architektura v Československu* [Modern Architecture in Czechoslovakia]. Praha: Odeon, 1930, pp. 226, 230.

151. Oldřich Starý, op. cit., p. 7.

152. *Byt a umění*, vol. 3 (1932), no. 5, pp. 105–113. The issue featured nine photographs of the house interior, but no text on the building.

153. In the 1930s Ladislav Žák published numerous articles that promoted the concept of collective housing, including: "Jak žijeme – jak bydlíme [How we live – how we dwell]." *Magazín Družstevní práce*, vol. 1 (1933–34), pp. 20–22, 53–55, 88–91. "Předobraz nového bydlení [A Model of the New Housing]." *Magazín Družstevní práce*, vol. 1 (1933–34), pp. 147–150.

154. Jiří Kroha, *Sociologický fragment bydlení.* Brno: Krajské středisko státní památkové péče v Brně, 1973. Karel Teige, *Nejmenší byt* [Minimum Dwelling]. Praha: Václav Petr, 1932. For a discussion of Teige's book, see the chapter "Architecture in Print."

155. Lubomír Linhart, *Sociální fotografie* [Social Photography]. Praha: Levá fronta, 1934.

156. See note 149.

157. Břetislav Štorm, *Architektura a pokrok* [Architecture and Progress]. Praha: Vyšehrad, 1941, p. 30.

158. Ibid.

159. See Edward Maufe, *Modern Church Architecture.* London: Incorporated Church Building Society, 1948. Photographs of the church appeared in *Stavba*, vol. 2 (1923–24), pp. 124–129.

160. See Edward Maufe, op. cit. and Břetislav Štorm, op. cit.

161. For a discussion of Plečnik's work, see Damjan Prelovšek, *Jože Plečnik 1872–1957.* New Haven and London: Yale University Press, 1997. *Josip Plečnik, An Architect of Prague Castle.* Zdeněk Lukeš, Damjan Prelovšek, and Tomáš Valena, eds. Prague: Prague Castle Administration, 1997; and Peter Krečič, *Plečnik. The Complete Works.* London: Academy Editions, 1993.

162. Arnošt Wiesner, "O stavbě krematoria [On the Construction of a Crematorium]," *Horizont*, nos. 11–13 (1928), p. 35.

163. Ibid.

164. Ibid.

165. Josef Kittrich, Karel Hannauer, and Josef Hrubý, "Okno a osvětlení interiéru [The Window and the Lighting of the Interior]." *Stavba*, vol. 9 (1930–31), p. 86. Jan E. Koula, "Horizontální okno [The Horizontal Window]," *Stavba*, vol. 10 (1931–32), pp. 106–107. Emanuel Hruška, "O iluzi průběžného horizontálního okna [On the Illusion of the Ribbon Window]." *Stavba*, vol. 10, (1931–32), pp. 106–107. Vojtěch Krch, *Okno – součást budovy a obytné místnosti* [The Window – A Component of the Building and the Living Room]. Prague: Krch, 1935.

166. *Bohuslav Fuchs, Masarykův studentský domov, Brno* [Bohuslav Fuchs, The Masaryk Student Dormitory, Brno]. Brno: Fuchs, 1930.

167. See Rostislav Švácha, "Towards an Iconography of Czech Avant-Garde architecture." *The Artistic Avant-Garde in Czechoslovakia 1918–1938.* Jaroslav Anděl, ed. Valencia: IVAM Centre Julio Gonzalez, 1993, pp. 120–131.

168. Josef Chochol, "Světelná architektura Prahy [The Prague Architecture of Light]." *Věstník inženýrské komory*, vol. 8 (1929), pp. 120–123. For a discussion of Chochol's views, see Rostislav Švácha, op. cit., p. 130.

169. See *Art into Life: Russian Constructivism 1914–1932.* Richard Andrews and Milena Kalinovska, eds. New York: Rizzoli, 1990.

170. Rostislav Švácha, "Pešánek's Systematic Artistic Designs for Light Advertising." *Zdeněk Pešánek 1896–1965.* Jiří Zemánek, ed. Prague: Národní galerie, 1996, pp. 405–408.

171. Viktor Schück, *Čtyři expozice na jedné desce* [Four Exposures on One Plate]. In: *Magazin Družstevní práce*, vol. 1 (1933–34), no. 12, p. 295. For instance, see Hugo Häring, "Problémy světelné reklamy [The Issue of Light Advertising]." *Stavba*, vol. 7, no. 9, pp. 129–130 (reprinted from Bauhaus, vol. 2, no. 4).

172. Jaroslav Anděl, "Artists as Filmmakers." Op. cit., pp. 171–172.

173. *Ozářená Praha.* Praha: PVV, 1928.

174. The earliest architectural journal in the Czech lands was *Zprávy Spolku architektů a inženýrů v Království českém,* published from 1865 to 1901 (under the German title *Mitteilungen des Architekten und Ingenieurvereines in Böhmen* from 1866 to 1870).

175. See *Dvacet let Štencova grafického závodu 1908–1928.* Zdeněk Wirth, ed. Praha: Štenc, 1928.

176. For instance, see "Zahraniční tisk o Stavbě [Foreign Press on *Stavba*]." *Stavba*, vol. 2 (1923–24), p. 109. This article quoted the statement by the prominent German critic Paul Westheim who called *Stavba* an "organ which is found nowhere else."

177. "Náš názor na novou architekturu [Our View of the New Architecture]." *Stavba*, vol. 3 (1924–25), no. 9, pp. 157–158.

178. "Bez pozlaceného vozu [Without a Gilded Car]." *Stavitel*, vol. 7 (1925–26), p. 23.

179. Karel Teige, "Mundaneum." *Stavba*, vol. 7 (1928–29), no. 10, pp. 145–155. Le Corbusier, "Obrana architektury [In Defense of Architecture]." *Musaion*, vol. 10 (1930–31), pp. 27–32. Karel Teige, "Odpověď Le Corbusierovi [An Answer to Le Corbusier]." *Musaion*, vol. 10 (1930–31), p. 51.

180. The architectural journal *Stavba* dedicated two special issues to the exhibition, see vol. 8 (1929–30), nos. 1, 2.

181. *Výstava Za novou architekturu*, p. 59.

182. Besides the publication *Masarykův studentský domov, Brno* [The Masaryk Student Dormitory, Brno] (Brno: 1930), Fuchs also published *Veřejné ideové soutěže na pořízení návrhů na skupiny budov [...]* [Public Competitions for Creating Projects for a Group of Buildings (...)] (Brno: 1930); and *Několik ukázek novodobých školních budov* [Several Examples of Contemporary School Buildings] (Brno: 1935).

183. See note 123.

184. For illustrations see, Jaroslav Anděl, *Avant-Garde Page Design 1900–1950.* New York: Greenidge Editions, 2002, pp. 201, 230.

architects' biographies

Adolf Benš (1894–1982)

Studied at the Czech Technical University, Prague, 1913–14, 1919–23, and the Academy of Fine Arts, Prague, 1921–24. J. Gočár's Office, 1924–25. Own office, 1925–39. State Planning Commission, City of Prague. Member of Association of Academic Architects, Czech section of CIAM, and S.V.U. Mánes. Editorial board member of the journal *Stavitel*. Professor of Architecture, College of Applied Arts and Crafts, Prague, 1945–65. Selected buildings: School, Mladá Boleslav, 1926–28. Electricity Power Board (with J. Kříž), Prague-Holešovice, 1927–35. Novotný house, Bratislava, 1928–29. Czechoslovak Pavilion, International Exhibition of Heavy Industry, Liège, Belgium, 1930–31. Bridge, Loket, 1931. Airport, Prague-Ruzyně, 1932–34. Bridge, Děčín, 1933. Bridge, Písek, 1936. School, Fiľakovo, 1937. Villa Benš, Prague-Dejvice, 1937–38. Family house, Klatovy, 1939–40.

Bohumír František Antonín Čermák (1882–1961)

Studied at the Technische Hochschule and the Akademie der bildende Kunste in Vienna, 1899–1903. Own office, 1908–60. Founded and headed the Art and Crafts Workshops in Brno, 1910–33.
Selected buildings: Workers Accidents Insurance for Brno and Silesia (with R. Farský), Brno-Zábrdovice, 1910–12. Old American Bar, Brno city center, 1914. Universum Cinema, Brno-Černá Pole, 1915. Electric Engineering Pavilion, interior, Fairgrounds, Brno-Veveří, 1923. Trade and Commerce Pavilion and Outlook Tower, Regional Fairgrounds, Brno-Pisárky, 1927–28. Family house, Brno-Královo Pole, 1929. ASSO administrative building, Olomouc, 1931. Family house, Svatý Kopeček, 1933–34. Family house, Jihlava, 1934–36. Family house, Lutín, 1935. Family house, Prostějov, 1935–38. Own family house, Bílovice nad Svitavou, 1939.

František Čermák (1903–1998)

Studied at the Czech Technical University in Prague, 1922–27. Taught at the same school, 1927–28, 1934–39, appointed Professor in 1947.
Selected buildings: Office building

(with G. Paul), Prague-Smíchov, 1934–35. Sanatorium (with G. Paul and A. Tenzer), Vráž, 1934–35. Provisional Hospital, Prague-Motol, 1936–45.

Václav Dvořák (1900–1984)

Studied at the State Technical Trade School in Brno, 1917–21. Own office, 1926–28, 1928–32 (with A. Kuba), 1932–47.
Selected buildings: Family houses, Brno-Žabovřesky, Brno-Židenice, Brno-Královo Pole, 1929. Apartment buildings (with A. Kuba), Brno-Veveří, 1929–30. Apartment buildings (with A. Kuba), Brno-Veveří, 1929–31. Family houses, Brno-Královo Pole, 1930. Erich Rouč-ka Factory, Brno-Slatina, 1930–31. Apartment building, Brno-Veveří (with A. Kuba and V. Kubas), 1932–33. Apartment buildings (with J. Brázda), Brno-Veveří, 1933. Apartment buildings, Brno-Old Town, 1933. Own family house, Brno-Žabovřesky, 1937. Apartment building, Brno-Veveří, 1937. Apartment buildings (with J. Brázda), Brno-Veveří, 1938–39.

Jaroslav Fragner (1898–1967)

Studied at the Czech Technical University in Prague, 1917–22, and the Academy of Fine Arts in Prague, 1934–35. Own office, 1922–49. Joined Devětsil in 1922, S.V.U. Mánes in 1931, Union of Socialist Architects in 1933, and other associations. Professor, Academy of Fine Arts in Prague, 1945–67, Rector, 1954–58, Architect of Prague Castle, 1956–67.
Selected buildings: Children's home, Mukačevo, 1922–28. ESSO Power Station, Kolín, 1929–32. Fragner Pharmaceutical Works, Dolní Měcholupy, 1929–31. Tatra Car Showroom, Kolín, 1930–32. School, Těšín, 1930–33. Villa Budil, Kostelec nad Č. I., 1931–32. Villa Morák, Nespeky, 1932–33. ESSO Transformer Station, Kostelec nad Č. I., 1934. Merkur Insurance Building, Prague-Old Town, 1934–35. Villa Majerová, Nespeky, 1936. Villa Orlický, Nespeky, 1938–40.

Jindřich Freiwald (1890–1945)

Graduated from the Higher Building Trade School in Prague in 1910. Office of A. Balšánek. Studied at the Academy of Fine Arts in Prague, starting in 1913. Own office (with Jaroslav Böhm), 1921–45. Killed by an SS unit at the very end of World War II.
Selected buildings (with J. Böhm): Hus Congregation church, Nové Město nad Metují, 1932–33. Family house, Prague-Dejvice, 1933–34. Apartment building, Prague-Bubeneč, 1933–34. Department store and apartment building, Prague-New Town,

1938–39. Designed a theatre in Hronov and a series of bank buildings in Kolín, Železný Brod, Dvůr Králové nad Labem, Hronov, Police nad Metují.

Bohuslav Fuchs (1895–1972)

Studied at the Academy of Fine Arts in Prague, 1916–19. Office of J. Kotěra, 1919–21. Own office, 1921–23 (with J. Štěpánek), 1923–50. Joined S.V.U. Mánes in 1928. Member of numerous other associations, including CIAM and CIRPAC. Professor of Architecture, Czech Technical University in Brno, 1945–58.
Selected buildings: Café Josef Zeman, Brno city center, 1925. Avion, Viola, and Radun boarding houses, Luhačovice, 1926–27. Hotel Avion, Brno city center, 1926–27. Municipal Baths, Brno-Old Town, 1927. Own family house, Brno-Žabovřesky, 1927–28. Family house, New House Exhibition, Brno-Žabovřesky, 1927–28. Brno Pavilion, Regional Fairgrounds, Brno-Pisárky, 1927–28. School (with J. Polášek), Brno-Stránice, 1928. Masaryk Student Dormitory, Brno-Veveří, 1929–30. Vesna Vocational Schools (with J. Polášek), Brno-Stránice, 1929–30. Eliška Machová Dormitory, Brno-Stránice, 1929–30. Moravian Bank (with A. Wiesner), Brno city center, 1928–30. Municipal baths, Brno-Zábrdovice, 1929–31. Morava Sanatorium (partly with K. Erstenberger), Tatranská Lomnica, 1931. Zelená žába Baths, Trenčianske Teplice, 1935–36. Alpa Office Building, Brno-Královo Pole, 1936. Railway Station Post Office, Brno city center, 1938.

Josef Fuchs (1894–1979)

Studied at the College of Applied Arts and Crafts in Prague, 1916–20. Own office, 1922–33. City of Prague Construction Office, 1933–36. Joined the Architects Association in 1923. Member of S.V.U. Mánes and Czech Werkbund.
Selected buildings: Prague Sampler Fair Palace (with O. Tyl), 1924–28. Prague-Holešovice. Winter stadium, Prague-Štvanice, 1930–32. Villa Funk, Prague-Dejvice, 1932. Villa Přerovský, Prague-Libeň, 1934–35. Family house, Prague-Libeň, 1938–39. Sanatorium, Písnice, 1940.

František Lydie Gahura (1891–1958)

Studied at the College of Applied Arts and Crafts in Prague, 1914–17, and the Academy of Fine Arts in Prague, 1918–23. Baťa Construction Office, 1923–46. City Architect of Zlín, 1923–26. Professor, Higher Building Trade School and School of Art, Zlín, 1938–45. Researcher, Institute of Architecture and

Urban Planning, Brno. Joined the Architects Association in 1923, and the Association of Academic Architects in 1928. Member of S.V.U. Mánes.
Selected buildings: Regulating plan of the Baťa Works, 1924. Masaryk Schools, Zlín, 1927–28. Baťa Department Store, Zlín, 1929. Big Cinema (with B. Martinec and Ing. Vtelenský), Zlín, 1931–32. Tomáš Baťa Memorial, 1932–33. Learning Institutes, Zlín, 1934–37. Zlín regulating plans, 1934, 1946.

Jan Gillar (1904–1967)
Studied at the Czech Technical University in Prague, 1923–25, and at the Academy of Fine Arts in Prague, 1925–28. Offices of J. Zázvorka, J. Kalous, K. Roškot, J. Krejcar. Own office, 1931–48. Joined Architects Associations, Association of Academic Architects, Left Front in 1929, CIAM in 1930, and Union of Socialist Architects in 1933.
Selected buildings: French Schools, Prague-Dejvice, 1931–34. Apartment buildings, Prague-Holešovice, 1936–37. Apartment building, Prague-Nusle, 1936–37. Teige house, Prague-Smíchov, 1937–38. Apartment building, Prague-Holešovice, 1937–38. Family house, Prague-Smíchov, 1939.

Josef Gočár (1880–1945)
Studied at the Higher Building Trade School in Prague, 1898–1902, and the College of Applied Arts and Crafts, Prague, 1903–05. Joined S.V.U. Mánes in 1905. Own office, 1908–45. Founding member, Group of Fine Artists, 1911, co-founder of the Prague Artistic Workshops, 1912. Professor, Academy of Fine Arts, Prague, 1924–39; Rector, 1928–31. Chairman, S. V. U. Mánes, 1931–38.
Selected buildings: Villa Jaruška, Brno, 1909. A. Wenke & Son Department Store, Jaroměř, 1909. U Černé Matky Boží House, Prague-Old Town, 1911–12. Sanatorium, Bohdaneč, 1912–13. Legiobanka Building, Prague-New Town, 1921–23. Tannery School, Hradec Králové, 1923–24. Czechoslovak pavilion, Exhibition of Decorative Arts. Paris, 1924–25. Grammar, elementary and council schools, Hradec Králové, 1926–27. Kindergarten, Hradec Králové, 1926–28. Ambrose Congregation of the Czechoslovak Evangelical Church, Hradec Králové, 1926–29. St. Wenceslas Church, Prague-Vršovice, 1927–30. Czech Railway Office Building, Hradec Králové, 1928–33. Villa Sochor, Dvůr Králové, 1928–30. District and Finance Offices, Hradec Králové, 1931–36. Villas at the Baba Settlement, Prague-Dejvice: Villa Maule, 1932, Villa Kytlica, 1932–33; Villa Glücklich, 1934; Villa Mojžíš-Lom, 1935–36.

Jaroslav Grunt (1893–1988)
Studied at the Czech Technical University in Prague, 1912–16, 1919. Masaryk University Construction Office in Brno, and State Construction Office, Regional Government in Brno, 1920–29. City Planning Department, Brno, 1929–58. Member of various associations, including The Architects' Club, Devětsil, the Group of Fine Artists in Brno.
Selected buildings: Family houses, Brno-Židenice, Brno-Stránice, 1923. Family houses (with J. Vaněk a S. Kučera), Brno-Černá Pole, 1923–24. Apartment building (with M. Laml), Brno-Ponava, 1923–25. Three-unit family house, the Nový dům colony, Brno-Žabovřesky, 1927–28. Masaryk Trade School of Continuing Education, Hodonín, 1929–30. Family house with furnishing, Brno-Stránice, 1935–36. Apartment building, Kroměříž, 1935–40.

Josef Hausenblas (1907–between 1941 and 1945)
Graduated from the Higher Building Trade school in Prague in 1927. Studied at Bauhaus, Dessau, 1927–28. Own office, 1930–39. Member of Devětsil, joined the Left Front in 1930. Participated in the exhibition *Film und Foto* in Stuttgart, 1929. Died in the war at the Russian front between 1941 and 1945.
Selected buildings: Terraced family-houses, Lenešice u Loun (partially realized), 1929–30.

Josef Havlíček (1899–1961)
Studied at the Czech Technical University in Prague, 1917–24, and at the Academy of Fine Arts, 1923–26. Office of J. Gočár, 1925–26. Office of J. Polívka, 1927–28. Own office 1928–36 (with K. Honzík), 1936–49. Founding member of Devětsil, 1920. Joined Architects' Association in 1923, Association of Academic Architects and CIAM in 1928, Union of Socialist Architects in 1933.
Selected buildings: Apartment buildings, Prague-Dejvice, 1925–26. Office building with stores (with J. Polívka), Prague-New Town, 1927–28. Habich Department Store (with J. Polívka), Prague-New Town, 1927–28. Czech Werkbund House (with J. Polívka), Exhibition of Contemporary Culture in Czechoslovakia, Brno-Pisárky, 1928. Villa Jíše (with K. Honzík), Prague-Smíchov, 1928–29. General Pension Institute (with K. Honzík), Prague-Žižkov, 1929–34. Apartment buildings (with K.Honzík), Prague-Nusle, 1931–32. Máj Sanatorium, Poděbrady, 1936–40. Molochov apartment buildings, Prague-Letná, 1937–38. Apartment building, Prague-Letná, 1938.

Karel Honzík (1900–1966)
Studied at the Czech Technical University in Prague, 1918–25. Own office, 1927–46 (1928–36 with J. Havlíček). Professor, Czech Technical University in Prague, 1947–66. Joined Devětsil in 1923, Architects' Club in 1928, CIAM and Left Front in 1929, S.V.U. Mánes in 1932, Union of Socialist Architects in 1933.
Selected buildings: Family house (with O. Starý), Prague-Břevnov, 1925–26. Apartment building (with J. Domek), Prague-Košíře, 1926–28. Langer family house, Prague-Podolí, 1929–30. Villa Jíše (with J. Havlíček), Prague-Smíchov, 1928–29. General Pension Institute (with J. Havlíček), Prague-Žižkov, 1929–34. Apartment buildings (with J. Havlíček), Prague-Nusle, 1931–32. Family house, Hradiště u Plzně, 1938–39. Laichter house, Dobřichovice, 1939.

Josef Hrubý (1906–1988)
Studied at the Czech Technical University in Prague, 1926–31. Own office (with J. Kittrich), 1931–46. Head of the Stavoprojekt office, starting in 1948. Joined Left Front in 1929, Union of Socialist Architects in 1933. Member of Architects' Club and other associations.
Selected buildings: Hus Congregation of the Czechoslovak Evangelical Church (with J. Kittrich), Ostrava-Zábřeh, 1933. School (with J. Kittrich), Březnice, 1933–34. School (with J. Kittrich), Neštěmice, 1937. Bílá Labuť Department Store (with J. Kittrich), Prague-New Town, 1937–39. Department store and apartment building, Prague-Vinohrady, 1938–39.

Pavel Janák (1882–1956)
Studied at the Czech Technical University in Prague, German Technical University in Prague, 1899–1906, and at the Academy of Fine Arts, Vienna, 1906–08. Office of J. Kotěra, 1908. Professor, College of Applied Arts and Crafts in Prague, 1921–42. Founding member of the Group of Fine Artists, 1911. Co-founder of the Prague Artistic Workshops, 1912. Founding member of Czech Werkbund, 1913, Chairman, 1924–39. Appointed Architect of Prague Castle in 1936.
Selected buildings: Hlávka Bridge, Prague-Holešovice, 1911. Family house, Jičín, 1911–12. Crematorium, Pardubice, 1921–23. Riunione Adriatica di Sicurtà (with J. Zasche), Prague-New Town, 1922–25. Villas Kafka, Filla, Beneš, and Benda, Prague-Střešovice, 1923–24. Škoda Works Office Building , Prague-New Town, 1925. Libeň Bridge, Prague-Libeň, 1924–28. Automobile Club, Prague-New Town, 1926–29. Airport,

Mariánské Lázně, 1927–29. Master plan and Villas Dovolil, Linda, and Janák, Baba Housing Exhibition, Prague-Dejvice, 1929–32. Hotel Juliš, Prague-New Town, 1928–33. Hus Congregation of the Czechoslovak Evangelical Church, Prague-Vinohrady, 1931–33.

Josef Kalous (1889–1958)
Studied at the Academy of Fine Arts in Prague, 1912–15, 1917–18. Office of J. Kotěra, 1918–23. Member of Architects' Association, S.V.U. Mánes and other associations. Selected buildings: Family house, Prague-Střešovice, 1926. Palace of Commerce and Industry, Regional Fairgrounds (with J. Valenta), Brno-Pisárky, 1927–28. Family house, Prague-Střešovice, 1931. ARA Boarding House, Prague-Smíchov, 1932–34. Interior Ministry (with K. Roškot and J. Zázvorka), Prague-Letná, 1935–39.

František Kalivoda (1913–1971)
Studied at ČVUT v Brně, 1931–33, 1935. Own office, 1936–50. Visiting teacher, School of Arts and Crafts, Brno, 1939–42. Selected buildings: Family house, Brno-Stránice, 1935–36. Savings bank (with M. Putna) Vsetín and Tovačov, 1938. Family house, Prostějov. 1938–40. Family houses, Prostějov-Drozdovice, 1939–41. Family house, Brno city center, 1940–43.

Vladimír Karfík (1901–1996)
Studied at the Czech Technical University in Prague, 1920–25. Office of Le Corbusier, Paris, 1926. Educational stay in the U.S.A: Office of Holabird and Root, Chicago, 1927. Office of Frank Lloyd Wright, Taliesin East and West, 1927–29. Head of Construction, Baťa Works, Zlín, 1930–46. Professor, Slovak Technical University, Bratislava, 1946–71. Guest Professor, University of Malta, 1978–82. Selected buildings: Regulating plans for the Baťa Works in Czechoslovakia and abroad, 1930–1946. Baťa Department Store, Brno city center, 1931. Společenský dům Hotel, Zlín, 1932–33. Baťa Department Store, Liberec, 1933. Apartment buildings and Společenský dům Hotel, Otrokovice. 1933–36. Own family house, Zlín, 1935. Baťa Film Studio, Zlín-Kudlov, 1935–36. Baťa Co. Towns East Tilbury, Great Britain, Belcamp, U.S.A., 1933–38. Baťa Department Store, Bratislava, 1936. Baťa Pavilion, World Exhibition, Paris, 1936–37. Family houses, Zlín, Otrokovice, 1936–40. Baťa Department Store, Amsterdam, 1937. Baťa Administrative Building, Zlín, 1937–38. Housing Estates Fučík, Zlín, 1946–48. Chemical Technology Faculty of Slovak Technical University, Bratislava, 1950.

Josef Kittrich (1901–1968)
Studied at the Czech Technical University in Prague, 1921–26. Assistant Professor, Czech Technical University in Prague, 1926–34. Office of F. Roith, 1934–36. Own office (with J. Hrubý), 1936–48. Professor, Czech Technical University in Prague, 1948–68. Member of Association of Engineers and Architects SIA. Joined the Architects' Club in 1930, and CIAM and CIRPAC in 1938. Selected buildings: School (with J. Hrubý), Přerov, 1930. School (with J. Hrubý), Březnice, 1933–34. School (with J. Hrubý), Neštěmice, 1937. Bílá Labuť Department Store (with J. Hrubý), Prague-New Town, 1937–39. Department store and apartment building (with J. Hrubý), Prague-Vinohrady, 1938–39.

Václav Kolátor (1899–1983)
Studied at the Czech Technical University in Prague, 191⁻–25. Construction companies, Prague, 1925–29. City of Prague Planning Commission, 1929–45. City of Prague Central National Council, 1949–59. Joined the Architects' Club in 1927, Left Front in 1929, Union of Socialist Architects in 1933. Member of S.V.U. Mánes. Selected buildings: Swimming pool, Prague-Barrandov, 1929–30. AXA Baths (with V. Pilc), Prague-New Town, 1930–32. Eva Swimming Pool (with A. Szönyi and F. Wimmer), Piešťany, 1934. Swimming pool, Česká Třebová, 1937–38.

Bohumír Kozák (1885–1978)
Graduated from Czech Technical University in Prague, 1909. Offices of O. Polívka and V. Nekvasil. Own office from the 1920s on. Joined the Association of Architects and Engineers in 1913, Member of Architects' Club in 1923. Editor of *Stavba*. Selected buildings: Switchboard Building, Prague-Žižkov, 1923–24. Masaryk Social Institutes, Prague-Krč, 1924–40. Department and office building with Avion Cinema, Prague-New Town, 1924–26. Tennis club, Prague-Letná, 1926. Maternal Care Pavilion, Prague-Krč, 1934–40. Assicurazioni Generali a Moldavia Generali Comp. building with Broadway Passage (with A. Černý), Prague-Old Town, 1936–38.

Emil Králík (1880–1946)
Studied at the Czech Technical University in Prague, 1899–1904. Office of A. Balšánek a O. Polívka, 1905–06. Professor, Czech Technical University in Brno, 1920–39. Member of Architects' Club, and Devětsil.

Selected buildings: Spa Hotel, Luhačovice, 1908–09. Theatre (with R. Kříženecký), Mladá Boleslav, 1909. Master plan, Regional Fairgrounds, Brno-Pisárky, 1923–24. Apartment building, Brno-Veveří, 1924. Administrative building of the Regional Fairgrounds, Brno-Pisárky, 1926–28. Café and Cinema, Regional Fairgrounds, Brno, 1928. Czechoslovak Tobacco Office Building, Brno-Zábrdovice, 1927–28. Western Moravia Power Plants' Heating Station, Brno-Zábrdovice, 1930–1931. General Insurance Institute, Brno-Veveří, 1930–32.

Josef Kranz (1901–1968)
Studied at the Czech Technical University in Brno, 1919–26. Office of J. Kroha, 1926. Office of B. Fuchs, 1927–29. Post Office and Telegraph Administrative building, Brno, 1929–49. Stavoprojekt, Brno, 1949–54. Selected buildings: Café Era, Brno-Černovice, 1927–29. Avia Cinema, Brno-Černovice, 1927–29. Family house, Brno-Žabovřesky, 1930–31. Family house, Brno-Černá Pole, 1930–32. Own family house, Brno-Černá Pole, 1933–35. Family house, Brno-Černá Pole, 1934–35. Family house, Brno-Žabovřesky, 1935. Boarding house, Budva, Yugoslavia, 1937.

Jaromír Krejcar (1895–1949)
Studied at the Building Trade School in Prague, 1912–16. Studied at the Academy of Fine Arts in Prague, 1918–21. Office of J. Gočár, 1921–23. Own office, 1923–33. Visit to the U.S.S.R., collaboration with M. J. Ginsburg, 1934–35. Own office, 1935–48. Professor at the Czech Technical University in Brno, 1945–48. Lecturer, Architectural Association in London, 1948–49. Member of Devětsil, and Umělecká beseda. Joined the Architects' Association in 1921, the Left Front in 1929, CIAM in 1930. Selected buildings: Villa Vančura, Prague-Zbraslav, 1923–24; Olympic Building, Prague-New Town, 1923–28. Family house, Prague-Strašnice, 1926–27. Association of Private Clerks Building, Prague-Vinohrady, 1927–31. Villa Gibián, Prague-Bubeneč, 1927–29. The U.S.S.R. Pavilion, Prague Sample Fairs, Prague-Holešovice 1928. Machnáč Sanatorium, Trenčianske Teplice, 1929–32. Czechoslovak State Pavilion, World Exhibition, Paris, 1936–37.

Jiří Kroha (1893–1974)
Studied at the Czech Technical University in Prague, 1911–16. Provincial Council, Kosmonosy, 1919–20. Own office, 1920–25. Professor, Czech Technical University in Brno, 1925–34, 1936–39, 1945–53. Member of

S.V.U. Mánes, Left Front, Union of Socialist Architects and other associations.
Selected buildings: Montmartre Bar, Prague, 1918. Regional Technical School, Mladá Boleslav, 1922–26. Apartment buildings, Kosmonosy, 1923–24. Bridge (with J. Farský), Kralupy, 1923–27. District Health Insurance Office, Mladá Boleslav, 1924–25. Gellnar Department Store, Mladá Boleslav, 1925–26. Exhibition of Northern Bohemia, Mladá Boleslav, 1926–27. Family house, Nový dům Exhibition, Brno-Žabovřesky 1927–28. Mankind and Its Birth Pavilion, Exhibition of Contemporary Culture in Czechoslovakia, Brno-Pisárky, 1927–28. Villa Kroha, Brno-Stránice, 1928–29. Family house, Brno-Stránice, 1935–36. Apartment buildings (with J. Bureš, V. Kuba and J. Polášek), Brno-Královo Pole, 1946–48.

Josef Kříž (1895–1988)
Studied at the Czech Technical University in Prague, 1914–23. Member of Association of Architects and Engineers S.I.A.
Selected buildings: Electricity Power Board (with A. Benš), Prague-Holešovice, 1927–35. Vokovice Depot Administrative Building, Prague-Veleslavín, 1932–35. Apartment buildings, Prague-Veleslavín, 1932–33. Stadium, Třinec, 1938.

Mojmír Kyselka (1902–1974)
Studied at the Czech Technical University in Brno, 1921–28. City of Brno Building Office and own office, 1928–52. Own office, 1962–74. Joined the Architects' Club in 1929. Member of Group of Fine Artists in Brno.
Selected buildings: Small-apartment buildings, Brno-Štýřice, 1927–31. School (with B. Fuchs), Brno-Židenice, 1929–30. Elementary School for Boys and Girls, Brno-Černá Pole, 1930–31. Schools (partly with J. Polášek), Přerov, 1930–34. Own family house, Brno-Staré Brno, 1932–34. Family houses (with E. Škarda), Brno-Stránice, 1935–36. Family and country houses, Brno-Bystrc, Vlkov, Babice, Lelekovice, 1936–45.

Karel Lodr (1915–1998)
Studied at the Building Trade School in Hradec Králové, 1930–35, and at the College of Applied Arts and Crafts in Prague, 1935–36, and at the Academy of Fine Arts in Prague, 1936–40. Offices of J. Gočár, J. Krejcar and P. Janák. He often used photocollages in his architectural, graphic and exhibition designs.

František Marek (1899-1971)
Studied at the Academy of Fine Arts in Prague, 1922–26. Member of S.V.U. Mánes.

Selected buildings: Apartment building with stores, Prague-Vinohrady, 1934–35. Family house, Prague-Záběhlice, 1936–38. Legiobank, Prague-New Town, 1937–39. Vinohrady Gymnasium (with Z. Jirsák and V. Vejrych), Prague-Vinohrady, 1938–46.

Otakar Novotný (1880–1959)
Graduated from the College of Applied Arts and Crafts, Prague in 1903. Own office (1904–29). Professor, College of Applied Arts and Crafts, Prague, 1929–54. Member of S.V.U. Mánes, Chairman. Active as a critic and theoretician.
Selected buildings: Štenc building, Prague-Old Town, 1909. Gymnasiums, Holice, 1908–11, and Rakovník, 1912. Apartment buildings, Prague-Old Town, 1919–21. Airport, Prague-Kbely, 1920–29. Apartment building, Prague-Holešovice, 1923–24. Czechoslovak pavilion, Venice, Italy, 1925. Municipal Savings Bank, Benešov, 1926. S.V.U. Mánes Building, Prague-New Town, 1927–30. Post Office, Louny, 1928. Villa Špála, Prague-Střešovice, 1931–32.

Gustav Paul (1903–1974)
Studied at the Czech Technical University in Prague, 1923–28. Offices of A. Engel, K. Roškot, and J. Blecha, 1928–30. Own office, 1930–48. After 1948 worked for state architectural offices, 1949–72. Joined the Architects' Club in 1928. Member of Umělecká beseda. Specialized in sanative buildings and participated in numerous competitions in this field.
Selected buildings: Administrative building, Prague-Smíchov, 1933–34. Sanatorium (with F. Čermák and A. Tenzer), Vráž, 1934–35. Apartment building, Prague-New Town, 1936–37.

Zdeněk Pešánek (1896–1965)
Studied at the Stone Masonry School, Hořicích, 1914–17, and at the Academy of Fine Arts in Prague, 1919–23. Studied architecture privately.
Selected works: Color Piano, 3 versions, 1922–28. Monument to Fallen Pilots, 1924–29. Light Kinetic Sculpture for the Edison Transformer Station, Prague-New Town, 1930. One Hundred Years of Electricity, 1930–36. Light advertising signage for the Löbl Department Store, Prague-Old Town, 1933–34.

Josef Polášek (1899–1946)
Studied at the School for Decorative Arts in Prague, 1921–24. City of Brno Construction Office and own office, 1925–46. Member of the Left Front, CIAM, Architects' Association,

and the Union of Socialist Architects.
Selected buildings: Funeral Chapel of City Cemetery (with B. Fuchs), Brno-Štýřice, 1925–26. School (with B. Fuchs), Brno-Stránice, 1928. Vesna Vocational Schools (with B. Fuchs), Brno-Stránice 1929–30. Apartment buildings, Brno-Husovice, 1930–31. Schools (with M. Kyselka), Přerov, 1930–34. Apartment buildings, Brno-Královo Pole, 1931–32. Apartment building, Brno-Černá Pole, 193–32. Alfa Sanatorium, Nový Smokovec, 1931. Own family house, Brno-Stránice, 1932. Moravian Bank, Boskovice, 1936. Low-income apartment buildings (with V. Kuba), Brno-Zábrdovice, 1937–38.

Karel Řepa (1895–1963)
Studied at the College of Applied Arts and Crafts in Prague, 1919–21, and at the University of Ljubljana, School of J. Plečnik, 1921–23. Office of F. Krásný, 1923–26. Own office, 1927–48.
Selected buildings: Museum of Industry, Pardubice, 1927–30. Fairgrounds for the Exhibition of Physical Education and Sport in the Czechoslovak Republic and its pavilions (City of Pardubice pavilion; Automotive pavilion and other industrial pavilions); Stadium (with F. Potůček), Pardubice, 1930–31. Red Cross Cinema (Jas Cinema), Pardubice, 1932–33. Kovařík Department Store and apartment building, Pardubice, 1934–36. Farmers Cooperative building, Pardubice, 1935–38.

Josef Karel Říha (1893–1970)
Graduated from the Czech Technical University in Prague, 1917. Office of J. Kotěra, 1917–18. Own office, 1923–48. Member of Architects' Club and Architects' Association.
Selected buildings: Apartment buildings, Prague-Bubeneč, 1923–25. A. S. Ferra Administrative Building, Prague, 1926–28. District government office, Strakonice, 1927–28. Báňská a hutní Administrative Building, Prague, 1928–30. Báňská and hutní apartment building, Prague-Dejvice, 1928–30. Own family house, Prague-Smíchov, 1929–30. Family house, Prague-Dejvice, 1934.

Čestmír Šlapeta (1908–1999)
Studied at the State Academy Fine Arts in Breslau, 1928–30. Own office (with L. Šlapeta), 1931–50.
Selected buildings: Villa Konečný – Paleček (with L. Šlapeta), Frýdek-Místek, 1931. Villa Pikulík (with L. Šlapeta), Kopřivnice, 1931. Villa Kotouček (with L. Šlapeta), Příbor, 1932–33. Villa Hilda (with L. Šlapeta), Příbor, 1933. Villa Chumchala – Nožička (with L. Šlapeta), Valašské Meziříčí, 1933–34. Villa

Hesse (with L. Šlapeta), Opava, 1934–35. Villa Klimeš (with L. Šlapeta), Opava, 1936. Alfa Cinema, redesign and adaptation (with A. Hošek), Ostrava, 1938.

Lubomír Šlapeta (1908–1983)

Studied at the State Academy Fine Arts in Breslau, 1928–30. Office of N. B. Geddes, New York, 1931. Own office (with Čestmír Šlapeta), 1931–50. Between 1950 and 1956 worked for state architectural offices. 1950–56. Own office, 1956–83. Joined the Architects' Association in 1932. Member of KVU Aleš in Brno, Moravian-Silesian Group of Fine Artists in Ostrava, Group of Olomouc Artists. Selected buildings: Villa Konečný – Paleček (with Č. Šlapeta), Frýdek-Místek, 1931. Villa Macourek, Frýdek-Místek, 1932–33. Villa Kotouček (with Č. Šlapeta), Příbor, 1932–33. Alfa Cinema, Ostrava, 1933. Villa Kremer, Hlučín, 1933–34. Villa Chumchala – Nožička (with Č. Šlapeta), Valašské Meziříčí, 1933–34. Villa Urbánek, Slezská Ostrava, 1933–34. Apartment building, Slezská Ostrava, 1935. Villa Martínek, Opava, 1935–36. Villa Liska, Slezská Ostrava, 1935–36. Villa Nakládal, Olomouc, 1936. Villa Mišauer, Olomouc, 1939. Theatre, Olomouc, 1941–42.

Antonín Tenzer (1908–2002)

Studied at the College of Applied Arts and Crafts in Prague, 1930–33. Office of J. Krejcar, 1927–34. Own office, 1934–37, 1939–44. Joined the Union of Socialist Architects in 1933, and S.V.U. Mánes in 1938. Selected buildings: Sanatorium (with F. Čermák a G. Paul), Vráž, 1934–35. Jalta Hotel, Prague, 1954–56.

Oldřich Tyl (1884–1939)

Studied at the Czech Technical University in Prague, 1903–09. Office of M. Blecha, 1909–12. Own office, 1913–34. Founding Member of the Architects' Club, 1913, Chairman, 1914–19. Founder and head of the Tekta Construction Cooperative, 1919–28. Co-founder and member of editorial board of *Stavba*, 1922–35. Co-founder and chairman, The New Prague Club, 1924. Selected buildings: Prague Sampler Fair Palace (Trade Fair Building) (with Josef Fuchs), Prague-Holešovice, 1924–28. YWCA Boarding House, Prague-New Town, 1923–29, rebuilt 1929–33. Academy Building, Prague-New Town, 1928–30. Shopping center and apartment building, Prague-New Town, 1929–30. Department store and apartment building with Bondy Passage (Černá růže), Prague-New Town, 1929–33. Garages, Prague-New Town, 1929–33.

Max Urban (1882–1959)

Graduated from the Czech Technical University in Prague in 1906. Own office, 1907–24. Founded ASUM film production company, 1910, director, screen writer, cinematographer. Designed a visionary plan titled *Ideal Prague*, 1915–18. State Zoning Commission, 1924–39. City of Prague Urban Planning Commission, 1939–49. Joined the Group of Fine Artists in 1911. Member of editorial board and Editor-in-Chief of *Styl* (1934–35). Member of S.V.U. Mánes. Selected buildings: Barrandov Terraces Restaurant, Prague-Barrandov, 1927–29. Masterplan of Prague-Barrandov. A-B Film Studios, Prague-Barrandov, 1931–34. Family house, Prague-Barrandov, 1932.

Jan Víšek (1890–1966)

Studied at the Czech Technical University in Prague, 1910–14, 1919–22. Representative of State Regulatory Office, 1924–26. Own office, 1926–49. Member of Devětsil, Association of Czech Architects and Engineers S.I.A., Architects' Club in Brno, CIRPAC and other associations. Selected buildings: Hus Congregation of the Czechoslovak Evangelical Church, Brno-Veveří, 1926–28. Family house, Nový dům Exhibition, Brno-Žabovřesky, 1927–28. UP Enterprises Department Store, Bratislava, 1928–29. Apartment building with store, Brno, 1929–30. Šilhan Sanatorium, Brno-Veveří, 1929, 1932, 1935. School, Chornice, 1932. School, Lomnice by Tišnov, 1936. Teachers' Dormitory, Brno-Veveří, 1936. District Government Office, Hodonín, 1936–38. Apartment building with stores and Luxor Café; Bratislava, 1937–38.

Arnošt Wiesner (1890–1971)

Studied at the Deutsche technische Hochschule in Brno,1908–10, and at the Akademie der bildende Kunste in Vienna, 1910–13. Office of Friedrich Ohmann in Vienna, 1913–14. Own office, 1919–39. Emigrated to Great Britain, 1939. Own office in London, 1945–48, Associate Professor, Oxford, 1948–50. Associate Professor, University of Liverpool, 1950–60. Selected buildings: Czech Union Bank, Brno city center, 1923–25. Crematorium, Brno-Bohunice, 1925–30, 1932–33. Café Esplanade, Brno city center, 1925–27. Family house, Brno-Stránice, 1926. Department store, apartment, and administrative building of Moravian Life Insurance Co. (Morava Palace), Brno city center, 1926–29, 1933, 1936. Family house, Nový dům Exhibition, Brno-Žabovřesky, 1927–28. Moravian Bank

(with B. Fuchs), Brno city center, 1928–30. Family house, Brno-Pisárky, 1928–29. Family house, Prague, 1930. Apartment building, Brno-Pisárky, 1931–32. Popper Department Store, Brno city center, 1931–32. Apartment building, Brno-Zábrdovice, 1931–33. Textile factories, Bielsko, Poland, and Lodz, Poland, 1935–38. Peraton Hotel, Kitzbühl, Austria, 1937–38.

Ladislav Žák (1900–1973)

Studied at the Academy of Fine Arts in Prague, 1919–24, School of Architecture, 1924–27. Own office 1930. Member the Union of Socialist Architects, 1933. Assistant Professor, garden architecture and landscape planning, Academy of Fine Arts in Prague, 1946–73. Selected buildings: Czechoslovak Ministry of Education, furniture, 1928–30. Villas Herain, Čeněk and Zaorálek, Baba Housing Exhibition, Prague-Dejvice, 1932. Villa Hain, Prague-Vysočany, 1932–33. Villa Frič, Prague-Hodkovičky, 1935–36. Villa Bárová, Prague-Dejvice, 1937.

photographers' biographies

Ateliér de Sandalo [Studio de Sandalo]
Rudolf [de] Sandalo (father) (1869–1932)
Rudolf [de] Sandalo (son) (1899–c. 1960)
Rudolf Sandalo (father) was the first chairman of the Society of Professional Photographers in Brno till 1918. In the 1920s and 1930s, he and his son specialized in architectural photography, being recognized as leading representatives of the genre. Their pictures of new buildings frequently appeared in both architectural journals and pictorial magazines, including *Salon, Měsíc, Index, Stavba, Stavitel, Byt a umění*). Sandalo Jr. moved to Berlin around 1940.

Ladislav Emil Berka (1907–1993)
Editor, film critic, photographer. Active as a photographer in the late 1920s and the first half or the 1930s. Influenced by the exhibition *Film und Foto* in Stuttgart (1929), he promoted the concepts of new photography and avant-garde cinema, and together with Alexander Hackenschmied and Jiří Lehovec, contributed to the development of film criticism. Editor of pictorial magazines *Ahoj* (from 1933) and *Květy*.

Jaromír Funke (1896–1945)
Photographer, theoretician, and teacher. A leading proponent of modern photography in the 1920s and 1930s. From the early 1920s on he followed the avant-garde movement, adopting some of its concepts in his work. Collaborated with leading architects Bohuslav Fuchs and Jaroslav Fragner in his pictures of the Masaryk student dormitory in Brno and the ESSO power station in Kolín. Was appointed to lead the department of photography at the School of Arts and Crafts in Bratislava (1931–35) and at the State School of Graphic Arts in Prague (1935–44). In its curriculum, among other subjects, he introduced an exercise that consisted in photographing modern architecture.

Jaroslava Hatláková (1904–1989)
Photographer. Graduated from the State School of Graphic Arts in Prague (1934–38), studied with Jaromír Funke. Her works from this period, which include pictures of modern architecture, advertising photographs and the series *Body in Space* [Těleso v prostoru] (1936), document a high level of photography education. Her pictures of General Insurance Institute in Prague that used oblique compositions and extreme perspectives were strongly influenced by Funke's work.

Svatopluk Innemann (1896–1945)
Film director and cameraman. Started in the movie industry as a cameraman during World War I. Authored thirty feature films in the 1920s and 1930s, many of which were comedies, including three films inspired by Jaroslav Hašek's novel *Good Soldier Schweik*. With cameraman Václav Vích made the documentary *Praha v září světel* [Prague in Shining Lights] (1928) that paralleled Walter Ruttmann's Berlin *Symphonie einer Grosstadt* (1927) and Dziga Vertov's *Man with the Movie Camera* (1929). With avant-garde writer Vladislav Vančura co-directed *Před maturitou* [Before the Finals] (1932), collaborating with other avant-garde artists, architect Bedřich Feuerstein and composer Emil F. Burian.

František Illek (1909–1969)
Photographer. Apprenticed with Václav Horn in Plzeň. Worked for the Centropress agency and with Pavel Altschul and Alexandr Paul cofounded the Press Photo Service, a leading agency in the field of commercial photography, in 1931. Known for his pictures of sport, architectural, and advertising photographs.

Jindřich (Heinrich) Koch (1896–1934)
Photographer and architect. Most probably the first Czechoslovak student at the Bauhaus (1922–28). In the 1920s worked in sculpture, design, architecture, and advertising. Studied photography with Hans Finsler at the Kunstgewerbe Schule Halle (1930–32) and succeeded him as head of the photography department (1932–33). After Hitler took power, returned to Prague, where he worked as a photographer for the National Museum in Prague (1934). Created the series of pictures of the ESSO Power Plant in Kolín (1933) and the Tatra Show Room in Kolín for the architect Jaroslav Fragner. Killed by a truck in an accident.

Bohumil Kröhn (1905–1992)
Photographer, chemist, lecturer. Studied at the Higher Technical Trade School in Prague, 1919–23, and at the Czech Technical University in Prague, 1923–28, Assistant Professor, 1928–34. Between 1934–43 owned a store specialized in photography, from 1943 on worked at the AB Studio film processing lab in Prague-Barrandov. His pictures, including advertising photographs, appeared in pictorial magazines between 1930 and 1945. Collaborated with the architect Vladimír Grégr.

Jan Kučera (1908–1977)
Filmmaker, critic, and theoretician. Member of the New Film Club (Klub za nový film, 1927), published numerous articles on film in avant-garde journals and *A Book on Cinema* [Kniha o filmu] (1941). In the 1930s employed by the Elektajournal newsreel agency, in 1937 became head of the Aktualita newsreel agency. In the early 1930s made several experimental films, including *Pražské baroko* [Prague Baroque] (1931), *Burleska* [Burlesque] (1932) and *Stavba* [Construction] (1932–34), which documented the construction of the General Pension Institute in Prague.

Jan Lauschmann (1901–1991)
Chemist, lecturer, photographer. Studied chemistry at the College of Chemistry and Technology in Prague, 1918–22, specialized in photochemistry, and worked for the Neobrom Co. in Brno, which produced photographic material (1925–48). Related to Drahomír J. Růžička, whose work had a great impact on him. In the late 1920s and in the 1930s also influenced by the new photography, frequently using oblique compositions in architectural photographs.

Jiří Lehovec (1909–1995)
Fillmmaker, photographer, film critic. Together with Alexandr Hackenschmied and Ladislav E. Berka, wrote on film and photography, emphasizing the significance of cinema for modern photography. Published his photographs in pictorial magazines (*Domov a svět, Světozor*). Member of the film and photo group of the Left Front, participated in the two exhibitions of social photography (1933, 1934) and the *International Exhibition of Photography* (1936) and the S.V.U. Mánes *Exhibition of Photography* (1938). From 1946 on taught at the Film Academy (FAMU) in Prague.

Karel Ludwig (1919–1977)
Photographer. In the late 1930s studied at the Baťa School in Zlín (1937) and worked for the weekly *Zlín*, taking pictures of Zlín architecture among other subjects. In 1940 moved to Prague, worked as an editor of the journal *Praha v týdnu*, then worked for the National Theatre and Lucernafilm (1943–48). His pictures often appeared in illustrated magazines. Became known for his photographs of nudes and ballerinas.

Jan Lukas (1915)
Photographer. Studied at the Graphischen Lehr- und Versuchsanstalt School in Vienna

in (1935–36). Worked as a cameraman for the Baťa Film Studio in Zlín (1936–1938). Frequently contributed to illustrated magazines, becoming a leading proponent of magazine photography. His series of pictures of the Morava Sanatorium (1931) represents an example of a psychological conception of architectural photography. Authored numerous pictorial books. Has lived in New York City since 1966.

Ada (Adolf) Novák (1912–1990)
Painter and photographer. Studied at the Academy of Fine Arts in Prague (1930–36). Member of the group Linie (1932–39) and the Association of Fine Artists of South Bohemia in České Budějovice (1941–49). Together with Josef Bartuška initiated the first exhibition of the group Linie (1932), which was dedicated to photography, showing among others a series of pictures of modern architecture in České Budějovice. His photographic style was inspired by the aesthetic of the snapshot.

Arno Pařík (1884-1958)
Owned studio specialized in advertising and documentary photography in Prague-Vinohrady (1925–39). Authored numerous architectural photographs, documenting new buildings.

Zdenka Pícková (1915)
Photographer. Studied photography at the State School of Graphic Arts in Prague between 1934 and 1938. Her work produced in this period includes photographs of modern architecture. Some of her pictures appeared in *Fotografie vidí povrch [Photography Sees the Surface]* (1935).

František Pilát (1894–1987)
Film technician, photographer, pedagogue. Studied at the Czech Technical University in Brno. Became a member of the Left Front in 1931 and participated in its exhibitions of social photography. As a photographer, also collaborated with Jiří Kroha on a series of photocollages *Sociological Fragment of Housing*. During his studies he made with Otakar Vávra *Světlo proniká tmou* (1930), a film on the Light Kinetic sculpture by Zdeněk Pešánek at the Edison Transformer Station in Prague (1930). In the mid 1930s was employed by the Baťa Film studio which he helped to build.

Karel Plicka (1894–1987)
Photographer, filmmaker, ethnographer, musicologist, teacher. Studied at the Teachers' Institute in Hradec Králové, 1909–13. In

1923 started to work for Matica slovenská to document folk culture, collecting songs, taking pictures, and making films (*Za slovenským ľudom*, 1929; *Po horách, po dolách*, 1930; *Zem spieva*, 1933). Created a series of photographs of the Zelená žába Baths in Trenčianske Teplice.

Jaroslav Rössler (1902–1990)
Photographer. Apprenticed with František Drtikol (1920). Member of Devětsil (1923). Between 1927 and 1935 lived in Paris. Pioneer of modern photography, influenced by cubism and constructivism in his pictures of constructions such as Petřín Tower and Eiffel Tower, light abstractions and photographs of cardboard constructions and photograms (1925). His photocollages and photomontages were indebted to Devětsil's picture poems.
In the late 1920s and the first half of the 1930s he worked in advertising photography, employing some of the devices used in his previous work. In the late 1950s he renewed his interest in special photographic techniques and further developed the aesthetic of his work of the 1920s and 1930s.

Josef Sudek (1896–1976)
Photographer. He apprenticed bookbinding (1911–13), lost his right arm during World War I (1917). Studied photography with Karel Novák at the State School of Graphic Arts in Prague (1922–24). With Jaromír Funke and Adolf Schneeberger, advocated new photographic trends in the amateur photographers club movement. In the second half of the 1920s and 1930s collaborated with Družstevní práce and Ladislav Sutnar, especially in the field of advertising photography. His photographs regularly appeared in Družstevní práce's publications, including *Panorama*, *Žijeme* a *Magazin DP*. Commissioned by leading architects (Josef Gočár, Jaromír Krejcar, Jaroslav Fragner, Vladimír Karfík), he often took pictures of new buildings. His later, more personal work brought him international recognition, making him the best-known Czech photographer.

Ladislav Sutnar (1897–1976)
Painter, graphic designer, art director, editor, teacher. Studied at the College of Arts and Crafts in Prague (1923). Professor of the State School of Graphic Arts in Prague (1923–39), and director (1932–39). Art director of Družstevní práce and designer of its publications. Pioneer of functionalist typography, often used photographs and photomontages. Exhibition designer of numerous

exhibitions, especially exhibitions of Czechoslovak architecture and design abroad. Edited (with K. Herain and O. Starý) and designed *Nejmenší dům* (1931). Lived in New York from 1939 to the end of his life, working as a designer. Recognized as the most important artist in the field of design in interwar Czechoslovakia.

Hugo Táborský (1911–1991)
Designer and photographer. Studied at the School of Arts and Crafts in Brno in 1927–32. Became a member of the Photogroup 5 (f5) in 1933, influenced by constructivism and surrealism. Used a variety of experimental techniques, for instance, melted photographic emulsion. Often employed photographs in his graphic design, especially for advertising.

Karel Teige (1900–1951)
Art critic and theoretician, editor, graphic designer, collagist. Co-founder of the artistic association Devětsil (1920), initiated the movement of poetism (1923) and advanced the concepts of modern typography. Edited *Disk*, *Stavba* and *ReD*. Co-founder and chairman of the Left Front (1929). Authored a number of publications on various subjects, including painting, photography, cinema, typography, and architecture. Recognized as the most influential critic and theoretician in Czechoslovakia. In the second half of the 1930s and in the 1940s made erotic photocollages, using photomechanical reproductions, including architectural photographs.

Josef Voříšek (1902–1980)
Construction engineer and car designer, photographer. Member of the Prague-Vinohrady Club of Amateur Photographers and several other clubs, member of editorial board of the *Fotografický obzor*. Produced fine examples of magazine photography. His architectural photographs and pictures from Paris were inspired by the new vision. In the 1940s was influenced by Josef Sudek, for instance, in the series on St. Vitus cathedral and the Lesser Town Cemetery.

Eugen Wiškovský (1888–1964)
Teacher, theoretician, and photographer. Influenced by *Neue Sachlichkeit*, followed Jaromír Funke in using oblique compositions. His pictures of the ESSO power plant in Kolín provide some of the best examples of architectural photography in Czechoslovakia between the wars. In the late 1930s produced landscape pictures that explored the concepts of Gestalt psychology.

selected bibliography

PERIODICALS

Architekt SIA. 26–43. Praha: 1927–1944, 1946–1951.
Architektura ČSR. 1–4. Praha: 1939–1942.
Časopis československých architektů. 21–25. Praha: 1922–1926.
Bytová kultura. 1–2. Brno: 1924–1925.
Byt a umění. 1–2. Praha: 1930–1932.
Disk. 1–2. Praha: 1923, 1925.
Horizont. 1–5. Brno: 1927–1931.
Forum. 1–8. Bratislava: 1931–1938.
Index. 1–11. Brno, Olomouc: 1929–1939.
Kámen. 1–21. Praha: 1919–1940.
Kvart. 1–5. Praha: 1930–1937, 1945–1949.
Magazin Družstevní práce. 1–4. Praha: 1933–1937.
Musaion. 1–2, 9–10. Praha: 1920–1921, 1929–1931.
Panorama. 1–17. Praha: 1922–1938.
Pásmo. 1–2. Brno: 1924, 1926.
Plán. 1–2. Praha: 1929–1932.
ReD. 1–3. Praha: 1927–1931.
Rozpravy Aventina. 1–6. Praha: 1925–1931.
Stavba. 1–14. Praha: 1922–1938.
Stavební rádce. 1–12. Praha: 1928–1939.
Stavitel. 1–19. Praha: 1919–1938.
Stavitelské listy. 1–38. Praha: 1904–1942.
Styl. 1–21. Praha: 1908–1938.
Tchéco–Verre. 1–4. Praha: 1934–1937.
Tvorba. 1–12. Praha: 1925–1937.
Veraikon. 10. Praha: 1924.
Volné směry. 1–49. Praha: 1897–1949.
Výtvarná kultura. 1–5. Bratislava: 1934–1938.
Výtvarné snahy. 8–11. Praha: 1926–1930.
Žijeme. 1–2. Praha: 1931–1932.
Život. 1–21. Praha: 1921–1948.

BOOKS AND EXHIBITION CATALOGS

Devětsil. Revoluční sborník Praha: V. Vortel, 1922.
Karel Teige, *Stavba a báseň*. Praha: Vaněk a Votava, 1927.
Fronta. Mezinárodní sborník soudobé aktivity. Brno: Edice Fronta, 1927.
Jaromír Krejcar, *L'architecture contemporaine en Tchécoslovaquie*. Praha: Orbis, 1928.
Zdeněk Rossmann, Bedřich Václavek, *Výstava moderního bydlení Nový dům*. (Exhibition catalog.) Brno: 1928.
Karel Honzík, *Moderní byt*. Praha: Kuncíř, 1928.
Karel Teige, ed., *Mezinárodní soudobá architektura*. Praha: Odeon, 1929.
Zdeněk Rossmann, ed., *Žena doma*. Brno: Index, 1929.
Oldřich Starý, *Rodinný dům na výstavě soudobé kultury v Brně*. Praha: Prometheus, 1930.
Karel Teige, ed., *Moderní architektura v Československu*. Praha: Odeon, 1930.
Karel Burian, Josef Hesoun, *Zařízení a úprava moderní kanceláře*. Praha: Sfinx Janda, 1930.
Exposition de l'art appliqué et de l'architecture tchécoslovaque. (Exhibition catalog.) Genève: 1930.
Tjeckoslovakisk arkitektur och konstindustri. (Exhibition catalog.) Stockholm: 1931.
Jan E. Koula, *Obytný dům dneška*. Praha: Družstevní práce, 1931.
Karel Herain a Ladislav Sutnar, eds., *Nejmenší dům*. Praha: SČSD, 1931.
Karel Herain, Ladislav Sutnar, Ladislav Žák, *O bydlení*. Praha: SČSD, 1932.
Karel Teige, *Nejmenší byt*. Praha: Petr, 1932.
Výstava bydlení: stavba osady Baba. Praha: SČSD, 1932.
Bohuslav Fuchs, Jaroslav Oplt, Zdeněk Rossmann, *Katalog výstavy stavebnictví a bydlení*. (Exhibition catalog.) Brno: 1933.
Jaromír Krejcar, *Lázeňský dům*. Praha: Knihovna lázeňské techniky, 1933.
Pavel Janák, *Sto let obytného domu nájemného v Praze*. Praha: 1933.
Alois Mikuškovic, *Technika stavby měst*. Praha: Klub architektů, 1933.
Oldřich Starý, *Architektura a stavebnictví ve XX. století*. Praha: 1933.
Karel Teige, ed., *Za socialistickou architekturu*. Praha: Levá fronta, 1933.
Bohumil Hypšman, Pavel Janák, Zdeněk Wirth, *Jak rostla Praha*. Praha: 1933.
Pracovní architektonická skupina [Karel Janů, Jiří Štursa, Jiří Voženílek], *Architektura a společnost*. Praha: 1933.
Josef Grus et al., *Byt. Sborník Svazu československého díla*. Praha: Petr, 1934.
Josef Havlíček, Karel Honzík, *Plánování a stavba Všeobecného penzijního ústavu v Praze*. Praha: Sdružení architektů, 1935.
Bohuslav Fuchs, Jindřich Kumpošt, *Cesta k hospodářské obrodě ČSR*. Brno: 1935.
Brno. Přehled historického, hospodářského, sociálního a stavebního rozvoje. Brno: 1935.
Alex Hofbauer, Václav Kolátor, *Lázně. Stavba lázní, koupališť a plováren, jejich úprava a zařízení*. Praha: Ministerstvo veřejného zdravotnictví a tělesné výchovy, 1935.
Jindřich Halabala, Josef Polášek, *Jak si zařídím byt...* Olomouc: Index, 1935.
Bohuslav Fuchs, *Několik ukázek novodobých školních budov*. Brno: Fuchs, 1936.
Josef Kittrich, Josef Hrubý Obchodní palác Bílá labuť. Praha: Grégr, 1939.
Výstava Za novou architekturu. (Exhibition catalog.) Praha: Uměleckoprůmyslové muzeum, 1940.
Architektura. Práce českých architektů 1900–1940. Praha: 1940.
Jan E. Koula, *Nová česká architektura a její vývoj ve XX. století*. Praha: Česká grafická unie, 1940.
Zdenek Pešánek, *Kinetismus*. Praha: Česká grafická unie, 1941.
Ladislav Žák, *Obytná krajina*. Praha: S. V. U. Mánes a Svoboda, 1946.
Karel Honzík, *Tvorba životního slohu*. Praha: Architektura ČSR, Petr, 1946.
Emanuel Hruška, *Urbanistická forma*. Praha: 1947.
Karel Teige, *L'architecture moderne en Tchécoslovaquie*. Praha: Ministerstvo informací, 1947.
Vladimír Karfík, *Teória architektonickej tvorby (typológia budov)*. Bratislava: Štátne nakladateľstvo, 1951.
Vladimír Karfík, *Typológia budov pre dopravu, administratívu a distribúciu*. Bratislava: SVTL, 1955.
Otakar Novotný, *Jan Kotěra a jeho doba*. Praha: SNKLHU, 1958.
Oldřich Starý, ed., *Československá architektura od nejstarší doby po současnost*. Praha: 1962.
Karel Havlíček, *Ze života avantgardy*. Praha: Československý spisovatel, 1963.
Vladimír Karfík, *Nové smery vo výstavbe škôl*. Bratislava: Vydavateľstvo Slovenského fondu výtvarných umení, 1963.
Oldřich Dostál, Jiří Pechar, Václav Procházka, *Moderní architektura v Československu*. Praha: Nakladatelství československých výtvarných umělců, 1967.
Dušan Riedl, Bohuslav Samek, *Moderní architektura v Brně 1900–1965*. Brno: Svaz architektů ČSSR, 1967.
Iloš Crhonek, *Brněnské výstaviště. Výstavba areálu 1928–1968*. Brno: 1968.
Czechoslovak Architecture of the Twentieth Century. London: RIBA, 1970.
Zdeněk Kudělka, *Brněnská architektura 1919–1928*. Brno: Blok, 1970.
Štěpán Vlašín, ed., *Avantgarda známá a neznámá. I.–III.* Praha: Svoboda, 1970–1972.
Zdeněk Kudělka, *Vila Tugendhat, Brno*. Brno: Krajské středisko státní památkové péče a ochrany přírody, 1971.

Jiří Kroha, *Sociologický fragment bydlení*. Brno: Krajské středisko státní památkové péče a ochrany přírody, 1973.

Vladimír Karfík, *Administratívne budovy*. Bratislava: Alfa, 1975.

Jiří Hrůza, *Slovník soudobého urbanismu*. Praha: Odeon, 1977.

Vladimír Šlapeta, *Moderní architektura v Prostějově*. Prostějov: Okresní kulturní středisko, 1977.

Otakar Nový, *Velkoměsto včera, dnes a zítra 1918–1999*. Praha: Horizont, 1978.

Vladimír Šlapeta, *Praha 1900–1978*. Praha: Národní technické muzeum, 1978.

Alena Adlerová, Jan Rous, Alena Vondrová, *Český funkcionalismus 1920–1940*. (Exhibition catalog.) Praha: Uměleckoprůmyslové muzeum; Brno Moravská galerie, 1978.

Josef Pechar a Petr Urlich, *Programy české moderní architektury*. Praha: Odeon, 1981.

Tomáš Černoušek, Vladimír Šlapeta, Pavel Zatloukal, *Olomoucká architektura 1900–1950*. Olomouc: Krajské vlastivědné muzeum, 1981.

Otakar Nový, *Bautätigkeit in der Tschechoslowakei*. Praha: Orbis, 1983.

Vladimír Šlapeta, ed., *The Brno Functionalists*. (Exhibition catalog.) Helsinki: Museum of Finnish Architecture, 1983.

Eduard Staša, *Kronika moderní architektury Gottwaldova*. Praha: Svaz českých architektů, 1985.

Rostislav Švácha, *Od moderny k funkcionalismu*. Praha: Odeon, 1985.

Zdeněk Lukeš, *Praha 7*. Praha: ONV Praha 7; Národní technické muzeum, 1985.

Vladimír Šlapeta, ed., *Die Brünner Funktionalisten*. (Exhibition catalog.) Innsbruck–Wien: 1985.

František Šmejkal, ed., *Devětsil. Česká výtvarná avantgarda dvacátých let*. (Exhibition catalog.) Praha; Brno: Galerie hlavního města Prahy; Dům umění, 1986.

Marta Čermáková, ed., *Výběrová bibliografie z dějin české architektury a urbanismu*. Praha: Národní technické muzeum, 1987.

Vladimír Šlapeta, ed., *Czech Functionalism 1918–1938*. (Exhibition catalog.) London: Architectural Association, 1987.

Jiří Kotalík, ed., *Tschechische Kunst der 20er und 30er Jahre. Avantgarde und Tradition*. (Exhibition catalog.) Darmstadt: Mathildenhöhe, 1988.

František Šmejkal et al., *Devětsil. Czech Avant–Garde of the 1920s and '30s*. (Exhibition catalog.) Oxford; London: Museum of Modern Art; Design Museum, 1990.

Marcela Macharáčková, ed., *Užité umění 20. a 30. let v Brně*. (Exhibition catalog.) Brno: Muzeum města Brna, 1990.

Ladislav Foltýn, *Slowakische Architektur und die tschechische Avantgarde 1918–1938*. Dresden: Verlag der Kunst, 1991.

Vladimír Šlapeta, *Baťa: Architektura a urbanismus 1910–1950*. (Exhibition catalog.) Zlín: Státní galerie ve Zlíně, 1991.

Dušan Riedl, *Brněnská architektura 20. století*. Brno: Památkový ústav, Úřad města Brna, 1992.

Pavel Novák, *Zlínská architektura 1900–1950*. Zlín: Pozemní stavby, Nadace Studijního ústavu Tomáše Bati, 1993.

Zlínský funkcionalismus. Sborník příspěvků symposia konaného r. 1991 ve Zlíně. Státní galerie ve Zlíně, 1993.

Václav M. Havel, *Mé vzpomínky*, Praha: Nakladatelství Lidové noviny, 1993.

Zdeněk Lukeš, *Pražské vily*. Praha: Zlatý řez, 1993.

Vladimír Karfík, *Architekt si spomína*. Bratislava: Spolok architektov Slovenska, 1993.

Výtvarná kultura v Brně 1918–1938. (Exhibition catalog.) Brno: Moravská galerie, 1993.

Sborník příspěvků z konference MU: Brněnská věda a umění meziválečného období (1918–1939) v evropském kontextu. Brno: 1993.

Jaroslav Anděl, ed., *The Artistic Avant–Garde in Czechoslovakia 1918–1938*. (Exhibition catalog.) Valencia: IVAM Centre Julio Gonzalez, 1993.

Jaroslav Anděl, ed., *Poezie pro všechny smysly. Meziválečná umělecká avantgarda v Československu*. (Exhibition catalog.) Praha: Národní galerie v Praze, 1993.

Michaela Brožová, Anne Hebler, Chantal Scaler, *Prague, Passages et Galeries*, Paris: Editions Norma a Institut Français d'architecture, 1993.

Alena Pomajzlová, ed., *Expresionismus v českém umění*. (Exhibition catalog.) Praha: Národní galerie, 1994.

Ivan Margolius, *Church of the Sacred Heart, Jože Plečnik 1922–33; Architecture in Detail*. London: Phaidon Press, 1995.

Rostislav Švácha, *Od moderny k funkcionalismu*. Praha: Victoria Publishing, 1995.

Rostislav Švácha, *The Architecture of New Prague 1895–1945*. Cambridge; London: MIT Press, 1995.

Ludvík Ševeček, Marie Zahrádková, eds., *Kulturní fenomén funkcionalismu. Sborník příspěvků konference*. Zlín: Státní galerie ve Zlíně, 1995.

Ctibor Rybár, *Ulice a domy města Prahy*. Praha: Victoria Publishing, 1995.

Miroslav Masák, Jiří Ševčík, Rostislav Švácha, *Veletržní palác v Praze*. Praha: Národní galerie v Praze, 1995.

Otakar Nový, *Ohňostroj pražských barů a lokálů, 1918–1999*. Praha: Protis, 1995.

Marcela Koukolová, *Ladislav Žák: vila režiséra Martina Friče*. Praha: CORA, 1996.

Ivan Margolius, *Prague: A Guide to Twentieth–Century Architecture*. London: Ellipsis, 1996.

Wojciech Leśnikowski, ed., *East European Modernism. Architecture in Czechoslovakia, Hungary and Poland between the Wars 1919–1939*. New York: Rizzoli, 1996.

Michaela Brožová, Anne Hebler, Chantal Scaler, *Praha, průchody a pasáže*. Praha: Euro Art a Volvox Globator, 1997.

Vladimír Šlapeta, *Baustelle Tschechische Republik*. (Exhibition catalogue.) Berlin: Akademie der Künste, 1997.

Satelity funkcionalistického Zlína. Zlín: Státní galerie, 1998.

Michal Kohout, Stephan Templ, eds., *Praha: architektura XX. století*. Praha: Zlatý řez, 1998.

Otakar Nový, *Česká architektonická avantgarda*. Praha: Prostor, 1998.

Zdeněk Lukeš, *Pavel Janák: vlastní rodinný dům Janák*. Praha: CORA, 1998.

Pavel Halík, Petr Kratochvíl, Otakar Nový, *Architektura a město. Studie*. Praha: Academia, 1998.

Jiří Hilmera, *Česká divadelní architektura*. Praha: Divadelní ústav, 1999.

Eve Blau, Monica Platzer, *Zrození metropole a moderní architektura a město ve střední Evropě 1890–1937*. (Exhibition catalog.) Praha: Obecní dům, 1999.

Oldřich Ševčík, *Programy a prohlášení architektů 20. století. Paralelní texty ke studiu dějin a teorie architektury*. Praha: ČVUT, Fakulta architektury, 1999.

Stephan Templ, *Baba. Die Werkbundsiedlung Prag*. Basel: Birkhäuser, 1999.

Jaroslav Halada, Milan Hlavačka, *Světové výstavy. Od Londýna 1851 po Hannover 2000*. Praha: Libri, 2000.

Marie Benešová, František Toman, Jan Jakl, *Salón republiky: moderní architektura Hradce Králové*. Hradec Králové: Garamon, 2000.

Zdeněk Kudělka, Jindřich Chatrný, ed., *O nové Brno. Brněnská architektura 1919–1938*. (Exhibition catalog.) Brno: Muzeum města Brna, 2000.

Tomáš Šenberger, Vladimír Šlapeta, Petr Urlich, *Osada Baba. Plány a modely*. Praha: Fakulta architektury ČVUT v Praze, 2000.

Jan E. Svoboda, Jindřich Noll, Ester Havlová, *Praha 1919–1940. Kapitoly o meziválečné architektuře*. Praha: Libri, 2000.

Karel Ksandr, Petr Urlich, Václav Girsa, *Müllerova vila*. Praha: Argo, 2000.

Petr Pelčák, Jan Sapák, Ivan Wahla, eds., *Brněnští židovští architekti 1919 a 1939*. (Exhibition catalog.) Brno: Spolek architektů, Obecní dům, 2000.

Rostislav Švácha et al., *Forma sleduje vědu. Teige, Gillar a evropský vědecký funkcionalismus 1922–1948*. (Exhibition catalog.) Praha: Galerie Jaroslava Fragnera, 2000.

Stephan Templ, *Baba. Osada Svazu čs. díla Praha*. Praha: Zlatý řez, 2000.

Milan Rak, *Architektura 20. století ve východočeském regionu z hlediska vztahu k historickému prostředí*. Brno: Vysoké učení technické v Brně, Fakulta architektury, 2000.

Adolf Loos a rekonstrukce Müllerovy vily. Praha: J. H. & Archys, 2001.

Vladimír Karfík, Vladimír Šlapeta, Milena Lamarová, *Frank Lloyd Wright a česká architektura*. (Exhibition catalog.) Praha: Obecní dům, 2001.

Zdeněk Kudělka, *Vila Tugendhat 1926–2000*. Brno: FOTEP; Muzeum města Brna, 2001.

Zdeněk Lukeš, *10 století architektury, Architektura 20. století*. Praha: Správa Pražského hradu; DaDa, 2001.

Avantgarda: vztah české a ruské avantgardy. K 80. narozeninám Jiřího Fraňka. Praha: Národní knihovna ER – Slovanská knihovna, 2002.

Zdeněk Lukeš, *Splátka dluhu*. (Exhibition catalog.) Praha: Fraktály, 2002.

Vladimír Šlapeta, František Musil, Václav Jandáček, *Funkcionalismus na Moravě*. Brno: Expo data, 2003.

Vladimír Šlapeta, Václav Jandáček, *Český funkcionalismus*. Brno: Expo data, 2004.

ARCHITECTS' MONOGRAPHS

Václav Dvořák
Jindřich Chatrný, ed., *Václav Dvořák, Alois a Vilém Kubové. Brněnští stavitelé 30. let*. (Exhibition catalog.) Brno: Obecní dům Brno, 2002.

Jaroslav Fragner
Otakar Nový, *Jaroslav Fragner, 1898–1967*. (Exhibition catalog.) Praha: 1969.

Jaroslav Fragner: Architektura. (Exhibition catalog.) Kolín: Regionální muzeum v Kolíně, 1991.

Jiří T. Kotalík, Jiří Novotný, Rostislav Švácha, *Náčrty a plány. Jaroslav Fragner*. (Exhibition catalog.) Praha: Galerie Jaroslava Fragnera, 1999.

Bohuslav Fuchs
Zdeněk Rossmann, ed., *Architekt Bohuslav Fuchs 1919–1929*. Basel: 1930.

Zdeněk Kudělka, *Bohuslav Fuchs*. Praha: 1966.

Mihály Kubinszky, *Bohuslav Fuchs*. Budapest; Berlin: 1986.

Pocta Bohuslavu Fuschsovi. Sborník referátu z mezinárodní vědecké konference v Brně. Brno: 1995.

Jan Sedlák, *Architekt Bohuslav Fuchs 1895–1972*. (Exhibition catalog.) Brno: 1995.

Iloš Crhonek, *Bohuslav Fuchs, celoživotní dílo*. Brno: 1995.

František Lydie Gahura
Ladislava Horňáková, *František Lydie Gahura: zlínský architekt, urbanista a sochař*. (Exhibition catalog.) Zlín: Státní galerie ve Zlíně, 1998.

Josef Gočár
Zdeněk Wirth, *Josef Gočár. Hradec Králové, Praha*. Wien; Berlin: Aida, 1930.

Zdeněk Wirth, *Josef Gočár*. Praha: 1947.

Marie Benešová, *Josef Gočár*. Praha: NČSVU, 1958.

Karel Honzík
Josef Havlíček a Karel Honzík, *Stavby a plány*. Praha: Odeon, 1931.

Josef Havlíček, *Návrhy a stavby*. Praha: 1964.

Životní dílo Karla Honzíka. Text J. Pechar. (Exhibition catalog.) Praha: Svaz architektů, 1967.

Josef Havlíček
Zdeněk Vávra, Radomíra Sedláková, *Josef Havlíček*. (Exhibition catalog.) Praha: Blok architektů a výtvarníků; Národní galerie v Praze, 1999.

Arne Hošek
Hana Rousová, Rostislav Švácha, *Arne Hošek*. (Exhibition catalog.) Praha: Galerie hlavního města Prahy, 1991.

Pavel Janák
Marie Benešová, *Pavel Janák*. Praha: 1959.

Pavel Janák 1882–1956. (Exhibition catalog.) Praha: Uměleckoprůmyslové muzeum, 1984.

Bohumír Kozák
Bohumír Kozák. Text by J. Bláha. (Exhibition catalog.) Praha: Melantrich, 1985.

Emil Králík
Iloš Crhonek, *Architekt Emil Králík*. (Exhibition catalog.) Brno: 1988.

Josef Kranz
Vladimír Šlapeta, *Josef Kranz 1901–1968*. (Exhibition catalog.) Olomouc: Galerie výtvarného umění, 1979.

Jiří Kroha
Jaroslav B. Svrček, *Jiří Kroha*. Genève: 1930.

Jaroslav B. Svrček, *Jiří Kroha, národní umělec*. Praha: 1960.

Výstava celoživotního díla národního umělce Jiřího Krohy. (Exhibition catalog.) Brno: 1964.

Josef Císařovský, *Jiří Kroha a meziválečná avantgarda*. Praha: NČSVU, 1967.

Rostislav Švácha et al., *Jiří Kroha*. (Exhibition catalog.) Brno: Dům umění města Brna, 1998.

Jiří Kroha: Kubist, Expressionist, Funktionalist, Realist. (Exhibition catalog.) Wien; Brno: 1998.

Jaromír Krejcar
Karel Teige, *Práce Jaromíra Krejcara*. Praha: Václav Petr, 1933.

Rostislav Švácha, *Jaromír Krejcar 1895–1949*. (Exhibition catalog.) Praha: Galerie Jaroslava Fragnera, 1995.

Miroslav Lorenz
Jaromír Krejcar, *Zlínská moderní architektura a pražská avantgarda*. (Exhibition catalog.) Zlín: Státní galerie, 1995.

Karel Lodr
Karel Lodr, Architektura 1938–1945. Návrhy, soutěže, plány a stavby. Praha: 1945.

Otakar Novotný
Jaromír Pečírka, *Otakar Novotný*. Genève: 1930.

Vladimír Šlapeta, *Otakar Novotný 1880–1959*. (Exhibition catalog.) Praha; Olomouc: Galerie výtvarného umění, 1980.

Josip Plečnik
Damjan Prelovšek, *Josef Plečnik, 1872–1957: Architectura perennis*. Salzburg: Residenz Verlag, 1992.

Petr Krečič, *Josip Plečnik: The Complete Works*. New York: Whitney Library of Design, 1993.

Zdeněk Lukeš, *Josip Plečnik: architekt Pražského hradu*. (Exhibition catalog.) Praha: Správa Pražského hradu, 1996.

Damjan Prelovšek, Eileen Martin, Patricia Crampton, *Jože Plečnik: 1872–1957*. London; New Haven: Yale University Press, 1997.

Damjan Prelovšek, *Josip Plečnik: život a dílo*. Šlapanice u Brna: Era, 2003.

Josef Polášek
Petr Pelčák and Ivan Wahla, eds., *Josef Polášek 1899–1946*. (Exhibition catalog.) Brno: Obecní dům Brno a Muzeum města Brna, 2004.

Karel Řepa
Štěpán Bartoš, Pavel Panoch, *Karel Řepa. Pardubický architekt ve věku nejistot*. Pardubice: Helios, 2003.

Čestmír Šlapeta, Lubomír Šlapeta

Pavel Zatloukal, ed., *Lubomír Šlapeta 1908–1983, Čestmír Šlapeta 1908–1999*. (Exhibition catalog.) Olomouc; Brno: Muzeum umění; Olomouc: Spolek Obecní dům, 2003.

Jan Víšek

Petr Pelčák, Vladimír Šlapeta, Ivan Wahla, eds., *Jan Víšek 1890–1966*. (Exhibition catalog.) Brno: Obecní dům Brno, 1999.

Arnošt Wiesner

Vladimír Šlapeta, *Arnošt Wiesner 1890–1971*. (Exhibition catalog.) Olomouc: Galerie výtvarného umění, 1981.

Ladislav Žák

Vladimír Šlapeta, *Architektonické dílo Ladislava Žáka*. Praha: 1975.

PHOTOGRAPHERS' AND GRAPHIC DESIGNERS' MONOGRAPHS

Ladislav Emil Berka

Antonín Dufek, *Ladislav E. Berka*. (Exhibition catalog.) Brno: Dům umění města Brno, 1992.

Jaromír Funke

Antonín Dufek, *Jaromír Funke: průkopník fotografické avantgardy (1896–1945)*. (Exhibition catalog.) Brno: MG Brno,1996.

Antonín Dufek, *Jaromír Funke*. Praha: Torst, 2004.

Jaroslava Hatláková

Antonín Dufek, Xavier Galmiche, *Jaroslava Hatláková*. Paris: Marval, 1988.

Antonín Dufek, *Hatláková/ Hatlák*. (Exhibition catalog.) Brno: Moravská galerie, 1991.

Jindřich (Heinrich) Koch

Karel Herain, *Práce Jindřicha Kocha*. Praha: SGŠ, 1935.

Jan Lauschmann

Daniela Mrázková, *Jan Lauschmann*. Praha: Odeon, 1986.

Jiří Lehovec

Karel Cudlín, *Jiří Lehovec, fotografické dílo z let 1929–1938*. (Thesis, FAMU.) Praha: 1987.

Antonín Dufek, *Aventinské trio (Ladislav E. Berka, Alexandr Hackenschmied, Jiří Lehovec)*. (Exhibition catalog.) Brno: Moravská galerie, 1989.

Karel Ludwig

Fotografie Karla Ludwiga. Praha: Čs. filmové nakladatelství, 1948.

Jan Lukas

Josef Moucha, *Jan Lukas*. Praha: Torst, 2003.

Karel Plicka

Martin Slivka, *Karel Plicka: básnik obrazu*. Bratislava: Fotofo, 1999.

Jaroslav Rössler

Vladimír Birgus, *Jaroslav Rössler*. Praha: Torst, 2002.

Vladimír Birgus – Jan Mlčoch, eds., *Jaroslav Rössler, fotografie, kresby, koláže*, Praha: Kant, 2003.

Vladimír Birgus – Jan Mlčoch, eds., *Jaroslav Rössler: Czech Avant-Garde Photographer*. Cambridge, Mass.,: MIT Press, 2004.

Josef Sudek

Anna Fárová, *Josef Sudek*. Praha: Torst, 1995.

Anna Fárová, *Josef Sudek*. Praha, Torst, 2003.

Ladislav Sutnar

Iva Janáková, ed., *Ladislav Sutnar – Praha – New York – design*. (Exhibition catalog.) Praha: Uměleckoprůmyslové muzeum; Argo, 2003.

Karel Teige

Rumjana Dačeva et al., *Surrealistické koláže 1935–1951*. Praha: Středoevropská galerie a nakladatelství, 1994.

Karel Srp, ed., *Karel Teige, 1900–1951*. (Exhibition catalog.) Praha: Galerie hl. m. Prahy, 1994.

Eric Dluhosch, Rostislav Švácha, eds., *Karel Teige, 1900–1951: L'Enfant Terrible of the Czech Modernist Avant-Garde*. Cambridge, Mass.,: MIT Press, 1999.

Karel Srp, *Karel Teige*. Praha: Torst, 2001.

Josef Voříšek

Vladimír Remeš, "Josef Voříšek, fotograf pro potěchu srdce." *Revue Fotografie*, Praha: 1973, no. 3.

Eugen Wiškovský

Anna Fárová, *Eugen Wiškovský*. Praha: SNKLU, 1964.

Vladimír Birgus, *Eugen Wiškovský*. (Exhibition catalog.) Praha: Pražský dům fotografie, 1998.

The New Vision for the New Architecture: Czechoslovakia 1918–1938
Jaroslav Anděl

Text © Jaroslav Anděl
Photographs © Anna Fárová, Zdena Kodíčková, Jiří Kröhn, Jan Lukas,
Jitka Panznerová, Arno Pařík, Miloslava Rupešová, Jana Slívová, Jiří Ströminger,
Štencův archiv, Sylva Vítová, Josef Voříšek, Helena Wilson, Dan Wlodarczyk.
For this edition © Scalo, 2006

Reviewers: Zdeněk Lukeš, Jana Tichá
Text editors: Richard Drury, Teresa Go
Lithographs: Art D - Grafický atelier Černý, Prague; Grafický atelier Degas, Prague
Graphic design: Šimon Blabla, Jaroslav Anděl
Printing: Trico, Prague

Illustration credits: Miroslav Ambroz, Jaroslav Anděl, Marie Benešová, Benjamin
Fragner, Karel Kerlický, Jaroslav Kořán, The Museum of Fine Arts, Houston,
Moravská galerie v Brně, Muzeum města Brna, Národní galerie v Praze, Národní
technické museum v Praze, nakladatelství Prostor, Sylva Šantavá, Vladimír Šlapeta,
Štencův archiv, Uměleckoprůmyslové muzeum v Praze, Josef Voříšek and other
individuals.

Scalo Verlag AG
Schifflände 32, CH-8001 Zurich, PO Box 73 / CH-8024 Zurich, Switzerland
tel +41 44 261 0910, fax +41 44 261 9262
publishers@scalo.com, www.scalo.com

Distributed in North America by Prestel, New York; in Europe, Africa, and Asia by
Thames and Hudson, London; in Germany, Austria, and Switzerland by Scalo.

ISBN-10: 3-03939-042-2
ISBN-13: 978-3-039390-42-7
Printed in the Czech Republic